DRUMS OF SUCCESS

10 STEPS TO TURNING YOUR
CREATIVE POTENTIAL INTO SUCCESS

A. Happy Umwagarwa

Drums of Success:
10 Steps to Turning Your Creative Potential into Success

Copyright © 2021 A. Happy Umwagarwa. All Rights Reserved.
Book cover drawing © 2014 by Visual Artist Strong Karakire.

No part of this publication may be reproduced, stored in a retrieval system, or transmitted, in any form or by any means, electronic, mechanical, photocopying, recording, or otherwise, without the author's written permission.

Published by

 Rainbow Pigeons Press

contact@rainbowpigeonspress.com

ISBN: 978-1-8382063-2-1 (paperback)
ISBN: 978-1-8382063-3-8 (ebook)

First published by Dog Ear Publishing in 2015

This book is printed on acid-free paper.

This publication is meant to be a source of valuable information for the reader. However, it is not intended to be used as a substitute for direct expert assistance. If such a level of assistance is required, the services of a competent professional should be sought.

This is a revised edition with more life stories from the author's creative journey. Names and other details of the people referred to have been changed to protect their privacy.

To Vivens, Bliss & Crissy Kalinganire

Contents

Foreword ix
Preface xiii
Acknowledgments xv
Setting the Stage xix

PART I: CREATIVE POTENTIAL

Step 1: Assess Your Situation 3
    Where am I? 4
    Is the world worth trusting? 8
    Am I allowed to be who I am? 11
    To what extent am I allowed to make mistakes? .13
    Do I need to change my situation? 18

Step 2: Discover Your Mental Capabilities 19
    Fluid intelligence and crystallized intelligence 22
    Different types of mental abilities 24
    How do we develop our mental abilities? 25
    Divergent thinking and convergent thinking 31
    How do our thinking processes
    affect our creativity 31
    Discover your mental abilities 34

Step 3: Understand Your Personality 37
   Are you inventive and curious or consistent and cautious? 39
   Are you efficient and organized or easy going and careless? 41
   Are you outgoing and energetic or solitary and reserved? 45
   Are you friendly and cooperative or skeptical and detached? 48
   Are you sensitive and nervous or secure and confident? 54
   Understand your personality traits 59

Step 4: Know Your Motivation Factors 61
   Passionate interest 62
   Personal drive 68
   Need satisfaction 71
   What motivates you? 74
   End of Part I—Your creative potential 74

PART II: CREATIVITY WORKSHOP

Step 5: Define Your Life Purpose and Set Your Goals 79
   Understanding your purpose and goals 82
   How to set goals 83
   Defining your life purpose and setting your goals 85
   To conclude on this 87

Step 6: Draw Your Strategies 89
   Essential elements of a strategy 90
   Unique personal message 91
   Personal brand and branding 97
   People and networking 101

Resources and finances..104
Draw your strategies 110

Step 7: Embark on Creative Production 111
Inspiration and idea generation..........................111
Visualization and illustration 116
Production and packaging..................................118
Release and distribution.....................................121
End of Part II 126

PART III: SUCCESS & SUSTAINABILITY
Step 8: Fight with Creativity Killers......................131
The Guru..133
The Perfectionist 136
The Sponsor 138
The Lover...143
Self...147

Step 9: Celebrate Your Success 150
What is success?...150
Self-realization...151
Social connectedness..152
Social responsibility..155
What is success, and how is it achieved? 157
Why and how to celebrate success 157

Step 10: Put Your Signature on the Future............163
Signature of excellence 165
Signature of inspiration......................................167
Signature of purpose 169

Conclusion 173
Supplemental Readings 177

Foreword

When I interview people about their work, a common response to my questions concerning creativity is: 'Oh, I am not creative, why would you want to speak with me?' Yet, in theory, every human being on this planet is capable of being creative. In fact, not only are we all endowed with creative potential, developing it is essential to our lives. We need it to solve not only our everyday problems but also the global issues causing us concern. Sadly, all too few develop their creative potential. This is not surprising. If we do not believe we are creative then it follows we will deny we have the ability. The question is, what world of discovery woul open up to us if we changed our beliefs?

Creativity simply involves bringing into being something new and valuable. After a little practice with divergent thinking skills it is possible to develop ideas that are completely new to us. If we keep practicing, and develop our knowledge, then we can start to see deeper problems that need fixing. Working on these problems can lead to novel ideas that have valuable and very practical applications. Starting out on the path to creative thinking is simple and you will have some quick wins.

The more you practice, the more effort you put in, the more complex and challenging it will get but persevere. You are on the path to discovering a world of possibilities.

There is a vast amount of knowledge being developed around the world about human creativity and we are beginning to understand and recognize many of the factors that can help develop our potential. Increasingly, we are able to bring this knowledge to the classroom and help others to learn these skills. Every year my students astound me with their inventiveness. They are capable of this not because they are especially gifted, or because of any unique teaching they receive, they do this simply because creativity is a capability we all have. Once we help them believe in and understand this ability, their imagination, ingenuity and creativity can fly. Which brings me to this wonderful book.

The wonder of human creativity is manifold. As you read this book you may be struck, as I was, by the beauty and wonder creativity can bring. This book, however, not only reveals techniques that can set you on your path to the creative life but seeping from its pages is a much more fundamental message. For me, this book revealed a deeply personal journey that demonstrates the power of human creativity to bring hope, wonder and magic to our lives, regardless of the circumstances we find ourselves in. If ever there was a recommendation for the true value of developing our creative potential it is this. Happy not only translates our understanding of creativity into some very useful and practical skills, she also shares her deeply personal creative journey through the examples she uses. These offer a perfect insight into the power of creativity to transform lives.

Creativity is a splendid thing. It shows us when our minds are free we can discover new ways of being and overcome the many obstacles of life. But keeping a free mind takes work. It is easy to become stuck in our ways, to rely on old habits and to believe the world cannot be changed. The lesson this book brings is simple. It is a lesson in hope. Free our minds and we can marvel at the possibilities to free ourselves. What are you waiting for?

Dr. Lee Martin
University of Nottingham

Preface

The purpose of Drums of Success is to provide you with ten simple steps to turning your creative potential into success. In addition to being useful to anyone who wants to understand the dynamics of creativity and its association to our everyday life; this book targets those who would like to discover their creative potential, put it to work to produce creative ideas and objects, and turn them into successful careers and businesses.

As part of my work as a Human Resources Professional for many years, I have advised organizations on fostering creativity in their employees, and, on the other hand, I have also provided guidance and counseling to individuals on their career success. I have realized that although there is a lot that should be done by schools and other institutions in terms of fostering creativity, there is also some need to look at other reasons why people with creative potential may not be putting it to work in their everyday lives and advise them how to do so.

In 2011, I started the quest to study how individuals can turn their creative potential into success. This book results from my research on both creativity and career or entrepreneurial success. The book does not focus on discussing creativity theories but gives the reader a simple guide to turning his/her creative potential into success.

In addition to stories from my professional experience as a Human Resources Professional and a Career Guidance Expert, in this revised edition of 'Drums of Success,' I have added life stories from my creative journey as a writer, novelist, storyteller, and poet. Whatever profession you are in, whether currently employed or have taken the path to be a self-employed entrepreneur, you will learn something from this book. You will discover your creative potential and how you can turn this into a success!

This book is useful for those:

Who would like to discover their creative potential and how to turn it into success in their lives. These need to read the whole book.

Who have discovered their creative potential but are not sure about what they should do to produce creative ideas and objects. These may read the whole book or start from Part Two.

Who have discovered their creative potential, produced creative ideas and objects, and would like to learn how to sustain their creativity and turn it into success. These may read the whole book or start from Part three.

Enjoy reading!

Acknowledgments

I am grateful to the Existence of the beautiful diversity that inspires me every second of my life. I thank Existence for giving me a mind to think, a soul to feel, and a body to act.

To Vivens, my husband. Thank you for your love. With your love, I can fly without any fear that I may drop and fall. You are there when I go, and you are there when I come back. Thank you for loving me the way I am: rebellious and independent. Only the strongest and the wisest man you are can handle the woman I am.

To my daughters, Bliss and Crissy! This book is one of the few gifts that I am giving to you. I will love seeing you developing your creative potential and turning it into success. I call you my little angels. You are the reason I keep moving!

To my late father, Canisius, the boy who was once given a pen by a priest, which he turned into the success that sent me to school. Those who murdered you thought it was the end; they did not know that you had already sowed the seed. I do not know if you can read this book, but if you do, know that I am grateful.

To my late mother, Thérèse: When you were working on the flower gardens, you thought that we would not notice. No. We were busy writing the process you were going through to turn your creativity into success. Thank you for being such a source of inspiration to me.

To the artist Strong Karakire, my younger brother. When I told you that you would be a coward because you had refused to complete your university studies, did you ever think that I would be the one listing you today as one of the people who inspired me to write this book?

Thanks to my siblings, John, Peace, and Queen. Thanks to my friends. Thanks to my colleagues. For your words of encouragement and for believing in me. Whenever you said, "Go for it, girl!" Whenever you said, "Yes, you can." You were pushing me to take another step forward.

Especially for this revised edition, I would like to thank all people who have supported me in my writing endeavors. I appreciate the readers of my books, short stories, and poems, as well as everybody who encouraged me with their positive or not-so-positive feedback.

Many thanks to all the people whose stories I share in this book. These shall inspire many readers who will decide to follow your footsteps and turn their creative potential into success.

Several people contributed many hours of their attention towards improving this book. Special thanks to Lori Conser and Sam Henrie for improving the formatting, style, and accuracy of the text. I would also like to express my gratitude Wheatmark team for their support during the re-publication of this revised edition of *Drums of Success*.

To all the young people, especially those in my home

country, Rwanda: You are a great inspiration. I have observed you every minute, trying to get out of the box, with just one purpose: to discover the heroes you are and let your heroism lead you to success. This book shall continue to guide you on the journey!

Most importantly, to you, who are reading this book and who have decided to take steps to turn your creative potential into success: All I can tell you is, "get moving!" The purpose of this book is to see you there!

Setting the Stage

When I was writing the first edition of this book, I thought I was speaking to others. Little did I know that I would be one of the people to be changed by the book I wrote. In 2018, my second book, 'Hearts Among Ourselves,' was published. It is neither a business nor an academic book. It's fiction, a love story set in the post-genocide Rwanda. If I had not written and read Drums of Success, I would probably not have decided to write a novel and share it with the public. It's not only the books that I have written and shared with the world. My poetry, which was my hidden refuge, is now shared with the public. I have learned to use my creative potential to express myself and contribute to making the world a better place with both prose and poetry.

Each of us has reasons why even the idea of coming up with novel ideas or products scares him/her. I also had my fears. I have always wanted to create something. I knew I needed to find my voice and make it heard. But I was convinced it wasn't going to be easy. The idea of throwing myself out to the world frightened me. Growing up till my early teenagerhood, people congratulated me on my creativity. I was a great singer and dancer, a member of a traditional dance group. I was a member of the drama team, as we called it, at my high school. I played basketball. I was a scout. I loved to express myself through writing. I used to write songs and share them with family and friends before throwing the paper away. I was interested in anything creative and loved to showcase my talents to those interested and those who were not. I would never have thought of these as desirable professions because, in my culture, they were regarded as hobbies. However, I was sure it made my life more exciting and wanted it to remain like that forever.

My innocent life changed in 1994 when my father and many other family members were killed during the genocide against the Tutsi. That's when I reflected on my life and concluded that the world was a horrible place in which to live. I decided all I needed was to survive. When the genocide was ended by the victory of the Rwanda Patriotic Front, a former rebel group, the storm seemed over. We had survived the worst of the tragedies of the twentieth century. However, life was not going to be the same again. How was our mother going to endure with her diabetes? Who would cater to her special needs? How about us? Our father, who was the only provider for the family, had been shot in both legs and buried alive. That's how they had decided to kill him. Our elder brothers were gone and murdered.

Our mother had nobody else to whom to turn. She had to do whatever she could to provide for us. She came up with different ideas. We joined a dance group, and Mama was among the singers, and we, the children, among the dancers. The money we earned from dancing was not enough. Since the day I opened my eyes, flowers have always surrounded me. It was my mother's passion. She collected flower plants and catered for them. She had never thought she could do gardening as a business and sell her precious flowers to other people. She had to provide for her children and other family members she had brought home to live at our house. She owed it to Papa and was not going to fail.

The story of my mother is similar to those of many other Rwandans. After the genocide against the Tutsi that took nearly a million people in 1994, everybody who survived was determined to live to accomplish a purpose. Some people had survived one of the worst atrocities the world has ever known, which meant that they were given a chance to live better than before. For some others, after experiencing the death of their parents, they found themselves playing the role of parents to their younger siblings as they did not have anyone to whom to delegate that role. They had to provide for and protect their younger brothers and sisters. Some others found themselves widows or widowers and needed to provide for their families, alone without their spouses. Some others had been refugees for decades, and it was their first time to live in a country they called their own. They left behind the possessions they had in some greener countries but with darker skies. It meant success, and they had to pursue that success. Many other Rwandans had seen their nation torn and destroyed in a few days and felt the drive to rebuild it.

For many Rwandans, the path to success was clear: to pursue formal education, earn a degree, and grab some of the job opportunities that were available in a country that had killed its intellectuals. It was the time that age was not a factor. Some children were in the same classrooms as their parents. Most individuals spent almost 20 hours a day for their self-development. After working hours, the traffic jam was not caused by rushing to go home, but to schools.

However, there seem to be new realities. Many young people, especially those in cities, continue to graduate with university degrees, but their numbers are far higher than the number of jobs created every year. Some have spent years without being able to secure employment. While some young people continue to focus on the job search efforts that may land them into their dream job, others have vowed to make it happen irrespective of whether somebody is willing to look at their resumes. These young people have started venturing in self-employment, requiring IT skills, business skills, and vocational skills, or industries of filmmaking, acting, music, visual arts, and others.

Strong Karakire, my younger brother, is one of Rwanda's young people who decided to take a different path. He started with dust and eye pencils, took a photo of our late father, and made his portrait. "Oh, that's Canisius! Oh, my God." That was my mother, nearly about to faint after seeing her late husband's portrait in her living room. I loved to know that Strong had a talent and enjoyed exploring his artwork until the day we had to have a family meeting to convince him to go to college. How did he dare to say that he did not want to go to college? He was going to be a coward. Oh! I was so afraid that my mother would have a heart attack. Strong did not have another option but to combine school with his art.

When I was pursuing a British Master's Degree

programme, and in the middle of my research on how performance is a function of mental abilities, personality and motivation, I received an email from my brother, Strong Karakire: "Happy, I love you. I love you all, my family. I love Mom, but I would like to let you know that I am dropping out of college. Please stop wasting your money on my studies…" How did I feel? I felt relieved. By then, I had realized my brother had found his element. He was already traveling to different parts of the world, including Europe, for exhibitions.

I believe I was also born creative. Yes, I was. I was born creative, independent, and rebellious until I was re-shaped to think inside a box. My teachers taught me that one plus one equals two and that it can never be three or eleven. I always waited for other people to make decisions about my life. One day I waited for my parents to tell me the school options that I was allowed to choose, and a few years after, I found myself with no possibility of doing a U-turn. That's how I ended up pursuing a Business Administration programme.

One day, for the first time in my life, I was allowed to choose, and I decided to specialize in human resources management. I did not know what it precisely meant. I just felt that it was going to be challenging. How can one claim to be able to manage human resources? Do we mean people? These are the most complex creatures to understand. I was going to find out how. I enjoyed studying their psychology; I enjoyed exploring how I can tap into their talents; I enjoyed learning how to develop their skills; I enjoyed studying how I can motivate and retain them. The most exciting part of my story is that I am still learning a lot about people. After many years as a Human Resources Professional for different private and public sector organizations, I am still pursuing my quest to discover more about people.

In 2010, I researched the criterion validity of psychometric tests used in the selection and development of human resources and concluded that performance is indeed a function of abilities, personality, and motivation. However, that research, instead of answering all my questions, it raised more curiosity. What do we mean by performance? I learned that it's about completing a task, an action, or a function. But that's not what I only wanted to find out. I wanted to understand more of our performance differences regarding the quality and result of what we do. I found the term: *Creativity*. It is about the originality and novelty of what we do. What's the link between abilities, personality, and motivation, on the one hand, and creativity on the other. Interesting! Creativity is also a function of abilities plus personality, a sum of which is multiplied by motivation.

I am from Africa, one of the continents with many less developed countries. Are people there not so creative? No. I have also been fortunate to go to other countries, and I remember the different beggars I saw on New York streets. There is no way we can say that these people do not have the potential to be creative. Yes, they do have it. What prevents them from turning this potential into success? What did successful people do best? How did they turn their creative potential into success? It was not difficult to know. I saw creativity at work in my own family. I saw creativity at work in my country. I saw creativity fostered and sometimes killed in the many organizations I worked for as a Human Resources Professional.

From both my educational and professional background, I have learned a lot about psychology and creativity. On the other hand, I have also learned a lot about entrepreneurship, business administration, and human resources management. It tells me much about the processes some people go through to achieve success. I have discovered that many people have found it difficult to cross over from just having the creative potential to succeeding in their careers and businesses. From 2011 to 2014, I examined what prevents individuals with the creative potential to use and turn it into success. Every single byte of knowledge, every unique life experience, led me to more findings, which I am pleased to share with you as I take you through the journey of turning your creative potential into success.

When I wrote the first edition of this book, I reflected on how my mother had turned her passion for flowers into a business that sent us back to school, and how my younger brother had proven that intelligence is not only measured by academic achievement and that once a person discovers his/her creative potential and decides to put it to work, success follows. I also shared in the book stories of other people who have made efforts to discover their creative potential, develop creative ideas, and produce innovative products. Apart from reflecting on my career choices, the book did not include much about my creative journey.

When *Drums of Success* was out in 2015, I received congratulations from my compatriots. I had done something great. I was invited by radios and TV stations to speak about my book. Interestingly, it seems as if most journalists were more interested in the stories I had shared in the book than the topic of creativity. Maybe stories tell more than theories, I concluded.

The fact that many people were interested in the stories I had shared in the book, especially about my mother and my younger brother, persuaded me to write a memoir or an autobiography. It was a small book of about 70,000 words. However, when I proofread it, I decided it wasn't probably the right time to reveal some details to the public. That's how I decided to write a fiction book instead. In 2018, my debut novel 'Hearts Among Ourselves' was published. The book has been out for almost two years. I even published one year later, a translation in Kinyarwanda. So far, I have only received positive feedback from Rwandan readers. I did not stop there. I have published close to ten short stories and close to twenty poems. All of these are about Rwanda and her people. My own life experiences inspire most of my poems. I like to call the short stories I write rainbow stories because the aim is to tell stories of different Rwandans, mostly those whose stories are too complex to fit into one narrative of the Rwanda history.

In this revised edition of Drums of Success, I'm not only talking to you as an expert, but also one of the people on the same creative journey many readers of this book are on and want to start. I'm sure you and I can learn and take the necessary steps towards success in our lives. I'm now a writer, novelist, and poet, and it's a profession I take seriously, even though I currently combine it with a full-time job as a Human Resources professional. There is more to being creative than producing creative objects and putting them out for the consumption of the market. I'm still on the journey to rediscover and recreate myself. I'm applying the tips shared in this book as one of the people who are on the journey to turn their creative potential into success. I have learned a lot not only about defining one's purpose but also about sticking to it. I have learned a lot about setting goals and strategizing. Many creativity killers have attacked me, and I'm on constant fight with them. However, I have also started celebrating success and signing in the future.

PART I

CREATIVE POTENTIAL

STEP 1

Assess Your Situation

Many people have the potential to generate creative ideas and produce innovative objects. Some people think this world's rules and dynamics make it difficult for them to develop creative ideas and objects. They don't master the world's systems and structures they should navigate through to achieve success. They don't trust the world. To them, the world is simply unfair and full of wicked people. Those beliefs have led to a sense of unworthiness, even in them. They concluded that, for survival, they have to adhere to what other people define as reasonable. They believe it's not allowed to be unique. They don't want to be labeled as weird and abnormal. They don't want to make mistakes and face the consequences. They don't want to try anything until they are sure nothing shall go wrong. Instead of coming up with novel ideas and produce innovative products, these people prefer repeating what others have already tried, tested, and approved.

In this first step towards turning your creative potential into success, I aim to encourage you to look into your situation, analyze the conclusions you have drawn about yourself, other people, and the world in general, and understand how these conclusions have affected your creativity success. I will conclude by giving you tips and hints on how to reverse the situation if you need to.

Where am I?

Babies, when they get out of their mothers' wombs, cry. Common sense tells me that probably when they come out, it feels cold. Maybe, they feel the void of a large space. Perhaps, the noise is simply unbearable. They are in a new environment and wonder if they will survive in that new world.

Since you were born, you have been trying to understand the world in which you live. You have sought to understand its dynamics, structures, systems, and laws. You have been seeking answers to these questions: Where am I? What are the norms governing behavior in this world? What structures should I go through when I want to act? What are the standards of performance accepted in this world? What does the world consider good or bad? Different factors influenced the opinions you formed about the world. These include your childhood family experiences, the environment you grew up in, the schools you went to, the difficulties you encountered in your life, the challenges you faced, the relationships you had, and all other good and bad experiences.

One day, I posted an article on social media. It was titled 'Journey to Career Success,' whereby I guided young people on what career success is and how they can achieve it. One person in my network posted a comment on my post, commending me for the message and agreeing with my career success approach. Then he added that there was only one thing that he disagreed with, and that was the fact that I had concluded my message by stating: "When you will give the world your best, it shall reward you." He wrote that I should understand that the world is imperfect and corrupt and does not always appreciate what is right.

Yes, I have also experienced unfairness in life, but I have also experienced fairness. Drawing an opinion of the world as unfair, imperfect, corrupt, cruel and any other negative conclusions, or on the other hand, looking at it from the other extreme of being very good, perfect, and trustworthy, are both results of the quest that we all started the day we were born.

I keep excellent memories of my childhood. I was born in a big loving family of eight children. My father was loving and caring, and so was my mother. It all changed in the year 1994 when I was only 15 years old. My father was murdered during the genocide against the Tutsi in Rwanda, and as we were still mourning his death, with no hope of surviving without him, our two elder brothers were also murdered. The world was indeed unfair to us, our diabetic mother, and our beloved country, Rwanda. I developed all sorts of negative thoughts about the world and its people. I did not know where and to whom to run. In one way or the other, that experience affected my life. It influenced my decisions as a teenager and adult, including those interpreted by my friends and relatives, as radical. It affected my mental models and led to how I define my purpose in this world.

The world offered me both the best and the worst. I experienced love from the world and its people, but I also received hatred from the same. On the one hand, this world's people abandoned me when I needed their warmth, but on the other hand, they wiped my tears during difficult times. The same society that killed my beloved father and brothers offered me the safety and security I needed to go through the painful experiences of being an orphan. The same world that was once at the hunt of my life whispered in my ears that there was still hope to live. The world offered me great opportunities in my personal life, marriage, career, and all other pillars of my life. I went through a lot. Sometimes, I felt resigned, and some other times, I felt energetic and ready to move mountains. Sometimes, I felt unworthy, and some other times, I felt like the best vengeance to those who made me an orphan was to live instead of just surviving. Sometimes, hatred beat me up, but some other times love rescued me. Sometimes, I felt oppressed, and some other times, I felt as free as a butterfly.

I am not encouraging you to see the world as perfect. You should simply see it as useful and pleasant. The world is diverse in nature, and this diversity is reflected in the countless colors of flowers and every aspect of life. The goal should be to live in harmony with this diversity. Learn to get inspired by diversity, explore it, beautify it, and make it better for current and future generations. If you considered the world a sphere, you would understand that there are so many ways to navigate through it and enjoy the journey. If you thought the world as a straight line, you would always live to search for that line and stay on it, and you will have different feelings of disappointment when things take a different course. If you want to achieve success in your life and experience the joy and happiness that comes with it, you will need to understand the world and its dynamics. You will need to appreciate the beauty of being in this world and the privilege of spending a century or a few more years enjoying the diversity of what this world offers to you.

Most successful people are those who have balanced opinions of the world. They do not see only one color. They can notice white and celebrate its purity. They can notice black and shade some light to it. They also notice some grey areas. They do not expect perfection; they pursue excellence. They do not only tolerate mistakes; they see them as learning experiences. They do not resent those who do evil; they shed some light on them and guide them towards the right.

It is not easy to be yourself when you are not sure if society values uniqueness and individuality. The only thing you search for when you are in such a situation is to fit in or to get out. You only seek ways to integrate or disintegrate. Most of us choose to comply, and that feels okay. Others decide to live as they please and end up rejected.

How do you find the balance? How do you comply and connect without giving up being yourself? You need to understand the world and its dynamics. You need to know how the world operates. You need to appreciate nature. You need to read people. Where do you get that realization from? The bad news is that it took you so many years to draw some conclusions about the world, either positive or negative, and if your judgments are not balanced, it may take you long to get the needed balance. The good news is that all you need to do is going back to the day you were born. Recall your childhood experiences. How about when you were a teenager or a young adult? Why do you see the world the way you do? How does that affect your everyday behavior? Speak to the world. Ask the world questions. Listen to it as it tries to respond to you, and hopefully, your judgment of the world shall find the right balance.

Is the world worth trusting?

In 2014, my siblings asked for permission to take my daughters out to a restaurant, and I accepted. When they came back, my brother told me that my daughter Crissy, who was then only three-years-old, had misbehaved. I asked them what she had done. They said to me that Crissy had decided to join a family on another table and share their food.

Crissy argued, "Mom, I was just sharing with my friends."

I knew what she meant because I always encouraged her to share with others. I understood the risks of trusting total strangers that much, but I did not know how to explain to Crissy that some people are untrustworthy.

I said, "Ah, You were sharing with friends! That's good! What are their names? Where do they go to school? How old are they?"

She did not have answers to these questions, and I believed I had succeeded in making her realize that she did not know those people well enough to consider them her friends.

Why did we all feel that she should not have trusted strangers to the extent of sharing food with them? Most people from my Rwandan culture would see this as an obvious question that calls for a straightforward answer. When I was eight years old, I accompanied my brothers to deliver a message from our parents to our uncle. It happened to be during lunchtime, and we left home before our lunch was ready. It was not far from our neighborhood, and the understanding was that we would come back and have lunch at home. Our uncle invited us to share a meal with him, but my brothers said we had already had lunch. I looked at them, astonished. When we left our uncle's house, I asked my brothers why they had told a lie.

"You never eat food from other people's homes," my brother replied.

I didn't reply but wondered if by 'other people,' he meant even our relatives.

Most people may argue that it has nothing to do with trust, and, understandably, you do not share your life with everybody. People should respect your space and never invade it. In my Rwandan culture, you do not expose eating habits. Drinking may be for social purposes, but not eating. The culture is now evolving with a lot of young people borrowing from other cultures.

However, my aim is not to discuss culture, but the underlying reasons we may have a lot of don'ts in our cultures. The main reason is that we believe that people are not trustworthy. We should not give them access to the full information of who we are, what we do, how we do it, and why we do it. You never know how they can use that information. People may harm us and our well-being. They do not wish us well and would do anything possible to stop our happiness, including poisoning our food to kill us or make us sick.

When we were infants, our basic needs were met mainly by our parents and other caregivers. These were not only physiological needs but emotional needs as well. When we were hungry, they fed us. When we were dirty, they bathed us. When tired, they took us to sleep. When sick, they treated us. People smiled at us. They talked to us. They interacted with us as recognizable members of their family or society. We learned to trust them. We concluded that the world was a safe and secure place. We smiled back and babbled sounds and words to interact with other people. The reality was different for the children who found themselves in the hands of absent, inattentive, neglectful, and or abusive caregivers. Instead of learning to trust, these neglected children developed mistrust. They concluded the world as unsafe and undependable, and this judgment affected how, as adults, they view the world and interact with other people.

Why is this important for the subject of creativity? Without trust, a person may develop new ideas, but it is only by trusting the world and its people that we will be free to express our ideas. The level of trust or mistrust is also a basis for evaluating the generated ideas and turning them into innovative products.

What should we do when the trust has been destroyed? The bad news is that once trust is destroyed, it's hard to regain it. The good news is that there are proven steps you can take towards regaining trust. You need to go back to the times you lost trust in the world. You need to analyze why and how it was destroyed. You should first focus on coming to terms with yourself. You should understand that you were once a victim of circumstances, but that does not mean your entire life should be of a victim. It has helped many people to talk about the events that destroyed their trust. I do not mean that it always has to be public or on national television, or that you have to write a book about it. You may do that if you want, and have weighed all the consequences of making it public. But the most important thing is that you go back to those times. I have seen adults going back to their parents and expressing how they felt as children if they remember. I have seen those who do not remember the life circumstances that led to the mistrust, but who took time to reflect on their life experiences and how these might have affected their judgment and behavior, talk about it, and make decisions to improve their situation.

Am I allowed to be who I am?

When you turned two years of age, your personality was characterized by emerging independence. You could see yourself walking like other people. You could eat by yourself, although it took long and some food was falling off your small spoon. When the potty was not out of reach, you used it before you wet your clothes. All these gave you a feeling of self-esteem and independence. Your next assignment was to prove to others that you are one of them. You said 'no' when they told you not to approach the TV set. You pushed your mother's arm when she wanted to feed you. They thought you were rebellious, and, indeed, you were. You tried to communicate to them that enough was enough. You could do it yourself. It was as if adults did not like that behavior. The older you grew, the more valued you were by your friends. They started inviting you to play. They loved your fantasies. You could sing for them. You could tell stories about your imaginary friends. You enjoyed being with your friends rather than being with adults. Yes, you knew you could go back to your mother whenever you needed to eat or sleep, or sit on her lap and feel relaxed. She was an excellent source of comfort for you. Life was getting more exciting! But one thing was puzzling you. Why did adults like to use the word 'no'? Why did they deny you to be yourself? Why did they want you to eat what they wanted and not what you wanted? Why did they want you to sit where they wanted and not where you wanted? Why could they not understand that you knew what you were doing?

You now understand why they forbade you to put a nail in a power socket. You realize why they did not allow you to cross the road alone. You know why they would not let you play with items that could harm you. You understand why they forced you to eat veggies and fruits when you only wanted ice cream. However, you fail to understand why they continue to control your life even now that you are a grown-up. You fail to understand why some people want to make decisions on your behalf. You guess that's how life is meant to be, and indeed you are right. Although we are individuals, we do not live in isolation. We live in families, communities, and societies with expectations of how we should think, feel, and act.

To what extent are you allowed to be yourself? To what extent are you allowed to do things your way? To what extent are you allowed to take your initiatives? To what extent are you allowed to decide where to be in terms of space and time? Whenever you have tried to do things your way, you experienced rejection from your relatives and friends. You never asked why. You did not ask why you had to attend a school and pursue a programme of studies that you never liked or picked. You never asked why they chose a religion for you despite the fact you did not quite understand its doctrine. You simply concluded that's how it should be.

It may be your artistic passion and talent that you would like to turn into a success story. Maybe it's about your ability to explore the dynamics of nature and deduce scholar-like theories. Perhaps it's about your ability to manipulate objects and create new tools. Is it about the verbal reasoning that makes you either a fantastic public speaker or writer? Is it about the exceptional reasoning capabilities that make you an incredible visual artist, a designer, an architect, or a photographer? Creativity is the ability to express one's personality and motivation through the production of novel ideas and objects. As much as it's vital to adhere to the societal norms, you can never effectively contribute to making this world a better place if you do not embrace your uniqueness and individuality. Do never aspire to be any other person but yourself. You have a lot to offer to the world.

To what extent am I allowed to make mistakes?

In my experience as a Human Resources Professional, I help organizations pick the right people from the labor market. We often use competency-based interview questions to determine candidates' past performance, assuming that past behavior is a good predictor of future behavior. Sometimes, I wonder what I would have said if somebody had asked me about my achievements when I was ten years old. I would probably have discussed how I used to construct cars and airplanes. I would not forget to talk about the songs I wrote and the stories I invented. Yes, I would also tell them about the radios and watches I repaired. How about the play teams I led?

Did I construct a car? Yes, I did. It could move like a car. It had wheels. And it is not only I who believed it was a real car. My friends wished they had one like that, and I volunteered to teach them how to construct their vehicles. Some parents begged me to build cars for their kids. How did I stop making cars? I stopped constructing cars the day adults told me my cars did not have an engine and were too small for any person to sit in and drive. They also reminded me of the fact that I could not construct cars without a degree in automobile engineering. If I had continued constructing my toy cars, maybe I would have made a model in which I could fit and drive, instead of pushing it like a wheelbarrow. Perhaps I would have found ways of using some energy sources to make my car move. I would probably have later discovered some model ideas which the most prominent car manufacturing companies would later adopt. Perhaps, looking at my cars, I would have come up with different ideas not related to vehicles. Maybe I would have become one of the famous designers or architects of today.

We should not be discussing mistakes when talking about creativity. It's all about the ability to come up with new ideas and objects. How can we call something new a mistake? What are we comparing it to? We would probably say that it's not yet meeting intended expectations and continue working on it.

My mother had a flower business. She did not only grow and sell flowers but also designed landscapes and made flower gardens for her clients. Occasionally, I accompanied her to work on her clients' gardens. I learned a lot from her creative process. She would start by drawing how the garden would look. The drawings could be changed several times before the clients approved the final proposal. Even after the work had finally begun, some new realities often led to the initial plan's change. Whoever would look at the garden on the third day of work could wonder what Mama was doing to that piece of land. After days of gardening, she would ask to receive her pay. I believe some clients wondered if the result was worth the hundreds or thousands of dollars they paid to her. She always offered the after-sales service, which was important. Otherwise, many gardens would never be green if not well maintained after the initial set up and planting. A few times, after like six months from the day she completed the work, I had the opportunity to go back with her to see the flower gardens she had made and take the photos we used for the business promotion. It was amazing to see the final product. Whenever I see some of the gardens my Mama made, I always stop and tell my friends that those marvelous landscapes with tall green trees are products of my mother's creative work. That's how creativity works. It's like sowing, and nobody should judge the seed but the tree and its fruits.

In most cases, we are not given a chance to go through the stages that my mother went through to make her flower gardens. We are judged when we are still at the idea generation stage. When we run to people to announce the 'I have an idea,' many people are quick to tell us how wrong we are. If a visual artist needs to write a proposal for his next art project in a very particular way, many of us would not understand. Unfortunately, for some of us we do not have the privilege that some artists have. We find ourselves in systems and structures that avoid mistakes at whatever cost, which affects our ability to turn our creative potential into innovative products.

One time, I approached a senior manager of the IT department of a company for which I worked as a Human Resources Professional. We needed to get an HR payroll software. The manager listened to me and stated that it would be on their to-do list for the following year because there was no budget. I asked her what she meant because I thought we had in-house capacities to do it. She told me nobody on her team had the skills to develop it. A few days after, I had a chat with one of the younger IT officers on her team about our needs and asked him what we could do in the meantime while waiting for the more sophisticated payroll system. The guy promised that he was going to do something. After three weeks, he took me through what he had already done, and I was astonished. It was not simple payroll software, but a tool for other tasks related to human resources administration. I decided not to talk about it before we had a final product. We input data, and for that particular month, we used it for our payroll. For the first time, the company produced payslips. When everyone started asking how we had done it, that's the time I revealed the name of the

IT officer. The company's top management recognized his achievement and decided to put his name on the hall of fame. If I had not made the mistake of interfering with that senior manager's decisions, which I usually don't do, a young talented person in the organization would not have gotten the opportunity to prove that he could do more than we thought he could. Was the head of the IT department wrong? No. She was only doing what we do in most organizations: avoiding mistakes and transferring risks associated with blunders.

Most people with a personal drive for creative work decide to quit their jobs and become self-employed. Some of these are later called in by the same organizations to do what they could never be allowed to do if they were full-time employees. I'm not suggesting we should all quit our jobs. However, the truth of the matter is that nobody can ever come up with anything creative if he/she is not allowed to make mistakes. I do not imply that you have to make mistakes to arrive at a novel product. I mean that it goes through an inevitable process that involves generating different ideas and plans. Some of these may fit in that particular space and time, and others may not. You go through a process of feeling it, touching it, and breaking it, and this process involves several breaks and makes. What leads you to the final creative product is the ability to enjoy that process of breaking and making and the commitment not to give up.

For some people, a mistake is an opportunity for learning and improvement. For some others, it's a reason to give up. Successful creatives are those who do not give up because they have made mistakes in their first attempts. The first product may be mediocre, the second good, and the third excellent. All we need to do is to learn from our mistakes and keep creating more and better-quality products.

Do I need to change my situation?

Now that you understand your situation, it's time to find that balance regarding how you view the world, people, life, and yourself. It's time to start understanding the dynamics of the world and appreciate them. It's time to start the journey to regain trust in the world, in the people, and more importantly, in yourself. It's time to start the journey to discover yourself, your abilities, personality, and what motivates you to do what you do. It's time to learn how to balance between adhering to the norms of the society and being yourself and doing things your way as an individual. It's time to change the way you view mistakes. It's time to start seeing mistakes as learning experiences. It's time to read the remainder of this book and discover your creative potential and turn it into success.

There shall never be one magical minute when you will immediately change how you feel about yourself, other people, and the world. There shall never be one magical minute when you shall say: "Wow! I am there!" It's a journey. This book aims to get you starting the journey and guide you in your quest to turning your creative potential into success. As a starting point, the next step is to understand the link between your mental capabilities and creative potential.

STEP 2

Discover Your Mental Capabilities

You probably have not dared to turn your creative potential into creative ideas and objects because you think you are not intelligent enough. Maybe it's because, in your childhood, your parents or other caregivers told you that you were suitable for nothing. It might also be because, in schools, you were not among those labeled as 'intelligent' because of their academic achievement. Perhaps you tried something, art, or sport, and when you failed to shine, you concluded you did not have what it took. My purpose is to help you realize you are intelligent and accompany you in discovering your mental abilities. I will not give you an intelligence test. I will simply encourage you to recall the moments when you experienced your intelligence at work.

What does intelligence have to do with creativity? There is no doubt that any creative process uses some brain functions. We all understand that we go through some cognitive processes when we analyze our surroundings. We think abstractly or logically on different uses and linkages, and generate new ideas on resolving various problems. But the question is, what mental capabilities correlate with creativity? What thresholds of these mental capabilities do we need for creativity? How can you discover and develop your mental abilities?

Another puzzling question that some of us have is understanding the link between academic achievement, intelligence, and creativity. You and I have seen people in our society who were best achievers in schools, but who, in their adulthood, have not proven the ability to generate creative ideas and produce innovative objects. To understand this phenomenon, we will define intelligence and discuss how it influences academic achievement and creativity. We all know that great students are traditionally capable of acquiring knowledge, storing this knowledge in memory, and applying the already stored knowledge to similar or different situations. The question is: How does that contribute to their creativity?

When I was in elementary school, academic achievement was never a challenge for me. In our school days, they ranked students from the best performer to the least based on our academic grades. They would call the first ten students in front of their fellow students, teachers, and parents, starting from the best student. Parents, teachers, and other students would applaud us. It was fascinating! I was always among the three best students in my class, and most of the time, the very best. This built confidence in me that I would achieve a lot in life. My father, who was also among the best, when he was still in school, always told me that he was proud of my academic achievements. But one thing troubled me. It was nothing else but the fact that Serge, my classmate, was far better than I was at drawing. I was able to get the highest grades in all other subjects but drawing. My highest score in art was 40%. It discouraged me, because

I could not understand why as intelligent as I believed I was, I could not draw.

Today, it's not about Serge, but my younger brother Strong, who has convinced me that academic achievement does not necessarily correlate with creativity. He has incredible artistic talents. I have been able to observe the process he goes through to get artwork completed. One day, I was walking with him, and then suddenly he told me to stop and wait. He had seen a stone. To me, it looked like a simple stone. As mountainous and rocky as my country is, we expect to see stones everywhere. My younger brother was so happy and started to show me how that stone was different from others. After a few days, he turned the stone into an incredible piece of art. What capabilities did Serge have that I didn't have? What mental abilities does my younger brother have that I may not have?

I'm a writer, and it seems writing comes somehow naturally to me. Apart from the fact that I enjoy writing, I want to think that I also have what it intellectually takes to be a writer. Does it mean that Serge and Strong excel in drawing and I excel in writing? Does it mean that we are all intelligent but with different mental capabilities? Yes. Today, I understand that the fact that a person can do something better than the other does not mean that the other person does not have something else in which he/she excels at. We all have different mental capabilities.

I may not be able to assess your mental capabilities. I aim to help you understand the different cognitive abilities and their relationships with creativity. I believe that after discovering your mental capabilities, nothing shall stop you from using them in your creative production. I will not give you an IQ test or some other aptitude tests. No. I will guide you in the process of discovering and recognizing your mental capabilities. Before discussing the cognitive abilities, let's define intelligence.

Fluid intelligence and crystallized intelligence

Intelligence is the ability to acquire and apply knowledge. When we say someone is intelligent, we often conclude so because he/she can comprehend some situations and concepts. On the other hand, we may refer to the fact that the person can apply skills, knowledge, and experience. We use intelligence to analyze problems, identify patterns and relationships, and extrapolate using logic. We also use intelligence to apply the already acquired knowledge. Scholars classify intelligence into two categories. The first category is known as fluid intelligence and the second as crystallized intelligence.

Fluid intelligence is the ability to think logically and abstractly. It is independent of acquired knowledge and does not develop through learning. Genetic factors influence fluid intelligence. On the other hand, crystallized intelligence is the ability to apply knowledge, skills, and experience. Educational and cultural backgrounds influence it. It employs the knowledge acquired from school and everyday life.

A high level of fluid intelligence may influence crystallized intelligence, but crystallized intelligence does not affect fluid intelligence. Both types of intelligence continue to grow steadily from our childhood through our adulthood. However, fluid intelligence peaks up more during adolescence, but starts to decline during adulthood, while crystallized intelligence continues to increase until late adulthood.

Why are we discussing intelligence, and what is the relationship between intelligence and creativity? As we stated before, creativity is defined as the ability to come up with novel ideas and objects. Although some scholars stated that there might be no correlation between intelligence and creativity, recent research has found that there is indeed a correlation between intelligence and creative potential. It all depends on the measurements used.

As earlier discussed, there are two types of intelligence: fluid intelligence and crystallized intelligence. We have already understood that fluid intelligence is the ability to think logically and abstractly. It is the ability to comprehend situations and identify problems and relationships. It's essential for creativity, for idea generation. It affects the fluency and originality of ideas. People with high levels of fluid intelligence can analyze what they see and think about linkages or new uses. On the other hand, crystallized intelligence is vital for the verification and evaluation of ideas. We tend to base on our experience and acquired knowledge to evaluate the validity and applicability of ideas.

We do understand that there is a relationship between intelligence and creativity. However, research proves that you do not need to have a very high IQ score, used to measure intelligence, to be creative. You should also understand that creativity is a complex phenomenon. It is not only influenced by mental capabilities, but also some personality traits. Intelligence is one of the elements that contribute to that creativity phenomenon.

Different types of mental abilities

There are so many mental abilities, and a lot of scholars classify these abilities in different ways. The ways we apply these abilities lead to various cognitive processes that result in particular intellectual productivity. In his multiple intelligences theory, Howard Gardner came up with the following eight mental abilities: musical-rhythmic and harmonic, visual-Spatial, verbal-linguistic, logical-mathematical, bodily-kinesthetic, interpersonal, intrapersonal, naturalistic, and existential.

You can understand that people like my brother Strong and my former classmate Serge may be applying more their visual or spatial mental abilities. With the example I have given before, you understand how Strong Karakire could see a stone and immediately visualize how it would look like a piece of art. These people can draw a big city like New York or Beijing on a piece of paper, and they don't need geometric tools to do so. On the other hand, those who apply more their verbal-linguistic mental abilities, like me, can remember, tell, or write stories. They can read and write. A lot of them will be more comfortable as journalists, writers, or public speakers. Those who apply their logical-mathematical mental abilities are more comfortable working with facts. These are people who do best as researchers and scientists.

The different mental abilities are linked to the functions of the two brain hemispheres, left and right. Although there is a misguiding myth that some people are either left-brained or right-brained, it does not mean anything else but just a tendency in our thinking. When involved in a cognitive process, many parts of our brain are involved, not just left or right. It's about the tendency. The same way, we tend to either use our right hand or left hand, our right ear or left ear; we also tend to use either our right brain or left brain. We all know that lefthanded people use both their left and right hands when involved in an activity. They simply have a higher tendency to use their left hand. The same applies to the use of the two brain hemispheres, left and right. In the past, teachers used to punish left-handed children. These teachers were wrong. Even though this may have affected the left-handed children's learning speed, they later managed to use their hands, at least for writing. They are still left-handed but trained to write with their right hands. This means that even people who are more comfortable with using their left-side hemisphere can also use the right-side, and vice versa.

What mental abilities are dominated by each of the brain hemispheres? The left-side of the brain is mostly used for cognitive functions involving logical and verbal abilities. On the other hand, the brain's right side is used primarily for cognitive purposes involving musical, spatial, interpersonal, and intrapersonal abilities. I want to underline the fact that there is nothing like some people are either left-brained or right-brained. It is a myth. The truth is that it is just a tendency. Some people prefer using more the left side or the right side of their brain. It means that logical thinkers can also have some musical abilities.

How do we develop our mental abilities?
Let's go back to the two categories of intelligence; flu-

id intelligence and crystallized intelligence. As we have already discussed, fluid intelligence increases by age and peaks up during adolescence. It starts declining during adulthood. On the other hand, crystallized intelligence continues to grow until late adulthood. We have understood that fluid intelligence is the ability to think logically and abstractly and is independent of acquired knowledge. We have defined crystallized intelligence as the ability to apply the already acquired knowledge, skills, and experience. We have understood that a high level of fluid intelligence may influence our crystallized intelligence. As we grow, we develop and sharpen our logical, linguistic, spatial, musical, kinesthetic, intrapersonal, interpersonal, and naturalistic abilities through our fluid intelligence to acquire knowledge and our crystallized intelligence to apply the acquired knowledge.

Parents, schools, and the environments we grow up in, play a significant role in the development of our mental capabilities. Parents and schools must focus on helping children and adolescents develop their cognitive abilities. In some cases, parents and schools do the opposite. Although this book focuses on what you, as an individual, should do, it's also essential to analyze the life experiences we went through that may have affected how we were able to develop some mental abilities. Those who are parents may as well understand that they should help their children develop their mental capabilities.

When my daughters were still very young, as their mother, not a psychologist, I could spot differences in their abilities. Some were justified by their age, and some others were affected by their inherent intelligence. My husband and I liked to say that one daughter talked, and the other acted. If one of them had broken a cup or had climbed on the bookshelf or was hiding behind the cupboard, we could quickly tell who that was. On the other hand, when I could not find one of my books, I would guess who had taken it to her room among the two daughters. Whenever I said something that I should probably not say in front of children, I could suspect who, among the two daughters, could repeat it to her friends. Does this mean that this is the same way they shall behave in adulthood? I do not know. So many factors shall come into play.

What should parents and schools do? They should give opportunities. Many schools, especially those that I have interacted with in Africa, have an academic curriculum that does not provide pupils and students with opportunities to develop different mental abilities. Most curriculums emphasize only learning how to read, write, and use numbers. I do not imply that this is not important. I am suggesting two things: Learning how to read and write words is only one of the elements that may contribute to linguistic ability. Even the development of this mental ability requires more than teaching children how to read and write words. Other elements include comprehending the uses and linkages between different concepts. The second point is that there is no superiority among mental abilities, and schools must not focus only on linguistic and mathematical abilities. Other mental abilities are equally important.

How do you tell the difference between the linguistic abilities of two three-year-old children who have not yet started school to learn how to write and read? It is more about their ability to understand the uses and linkages of words. Children with a higher linguistic ability already understand synonyms, antonyms, and even some hyponyms and homonyms. These children have never been taught this in school, but they have had, in their early years, opportunities to use their inherent intelligence to develop these abilities. What kind of opportunities have these children been given? For example, research proves that children develop the hearing faculty when they are still in their mothers' wombs. Mothers, who talk fluently to their children from when they are forming in the wombs through the infant age, allow them to develop linguistic abilities at an early age. It does not only affect their mental abilities but their self-confidence as well, which is equally essential for creativity and learning and development.

It is not only about linguistic abilities. It applies as well to other mental abilities. It's about knowing how to give children opportunities to develop these abilities. When my daughters were toddlers, I used to buy toys, which I did not understand how they worked. All I did was to check the age bracket appropriate for that particular toy. It was interesting to see how, in a couple of hours, a child could come up with different ways of using the toys. Parents may not need to buy expensive toys for their children. You may use some other items from our surroundings. When each of our daughters was at the age of crawling and making her first steps, I had a cabinet in the kitchen with her plastic plates and cups. These were not expensive to buy, but she was so happy because they were in the same shapes as those I was also using for my cooking. That occupied her and gave me time to focus on cooking. Another benefit was that she interacted with different colors and shapes, which is essential for both spatial reasoning and logical reasoning.

Likewise, schools should also give children in all age brackets the opportunities to use their fluid intelligence and crystallized intelligence and develop different mental abilities. There is a term that some schools like to use, which, in my opinion, misguide parents: Extra-curriculum activities. Most of these are even made entirely optional. These activities should be part of the curriculum. The school should only allow the students to choose from different activities in a particular group or for a specific period. They should never be labeled as 'extra curriculum' activities. They should be intentional and part of the academic curriculum.

I would like to come back to the link between academic achievement and mental abilities. In schools that focus on teaching students how to read and write, and how to use numbers, a student, like my brother Strong Karakire, a visual artist, may lose interest in studying. The reason would be that those who prove to have musical and spatial mental abilities are often not congratulated for their abilities. It does not mean that they cannot develop verbal and mathematical abilities. They simply prefer more to use the right side of their brain. Allowing these students to use their mental abilities may not only result in improved performance in music and visual arts but also in other areas of intelligence, including logic and linguistics. They develop more interest in studying. Students with musical, spatial, or other mental abilities should be as intellectually valued as those with linguistic and mathematical abilities.

I believe, by now, you understand that the fact that you did not have the highest academic achievement or that you were not excellent at numbers or reading does not mean that you are not intelligent. Are you probably one of those who were good at math or language, but who, as an adult, wonders why those who did not perform well in schools seem to be more creative than you are? I would like to tell you that maybe you have the potential to be creative, and all you need to do is discover it and turn it into creative ideas and products. However, you should also understand that the fact that you performed higher in schools is not a guarantee for creative success. Even those who did not score high in math and languages, had other equally valuable mental abilities.

Creativity is not a concept only associated with those labeled as "creative industries." Whatever mental abilities you have and whatever profession you have chosen, you can be creative. You should discover your cognitive abilities and embark on generating creative ideas and producing innovative products.

We have discussed the different mental abilities. We understand the creative products with which those cognitive abilities are associated. These include creative written work such as prose and poetry, mathematical concepts, songs, games, visual arts, etc. What we do not understand is the mental process that leads to these innovative products. The first way to sharpen and use mental abilities is through thought-development or thinking. Let's look at two types of thinking processes and how they affect our creative potential.

Divergent thinking and convergent thinking

Thinking is the human activity that generates or arranges ideas. We generate ideas through a thinking process. We engage in thinking to comprehend situations and surroundings. We also go through the thinking process to resolve different problems. Research has proven that we go through various thinking processes to analyze the causes of problems and generate possible solutions.

Divergent thinking is the process of generating many ideas on how a problem can be solved. It may also be about coming up with different assumptions about different causes of a particular situation. Convergent thinking, on the other hand, is the process of coming up with the most optimum way of solving a problem. Divergent thinking happens typically in a spontaneous free-flowing manner. Convergent thinking, on the other hand, maybe based on acquired knowledge, defined formulas, and standard procedures.

How do our thinking processes affect our creativity?

Our divergent thinking capabilities help with idea generation. They help us analyze situations by deducing possible causes of the problem and potential effects. A lot of creative thinking techniques involve divergent thinking. Companies that are known to be innovative increase their product line through some divergent thinking techniques. Through a divergent thinking process, they list clients' needs that they will want to satisfy and different ways to meet those needs. They come up with different combinations of products, from which the clients can choose.

On the other hand, as buyers, sometimes we go through some convergent thinking process to choose what to buy. Occasionally, we go for what we previously used and found useful. We may buy what was recommended by a friend, or we may just buy the cheapest items. The convergent thinking process involves making choices based on the familiar or already stored information or standard criteria.

Creativity is more linked to divergent thinking. It is about generating different novel ideas. Creative people can come up with new ways of doing things. Creative people always ask the 'what if' question. Creative people do not immediately conform to one way of doing things. It may be irritating to some people because divergent thinkers will always have ideas on how things can be done differently. On the other hand, people who prefer convergent thinking hesitate to take risks. They prefer applying proven methods of solving problems. It is more difficult for them to accept and adapt to change.

In most cases, convergent thinking is used in conjunction with divergent thinking. We usually tune to our free-flow mode to engage in a divergent thinking process, and once we have a lot of ideas, we switch back to our restrained mode to engage in a convergent thinking process. For example, a good guy at manipulating computers and developing software may be in a market observing the transactions people make. He reflects on the possible ways information technology can make their life easier. Ideas continue to flow in his little head. He goes home, takes his computer, probably to do something else, but he continues to visualize what he has seen in the market, and ideas continue to flow on how he can help these people. He types down some of these ideas. He even tries to manipulate some of the tools he has on his computer. He is not clear about what he is doing. It just feels interesting! This guy can do this for days, months, or years. It is what a divergent thinking process is about. As he continues to generate different ideas, he concludes that there are various ways he could help these people in the market do their transactions in more comfortable and efficient manner. He has a long list. This guy shall need to switch to his restrained mode to concentrate on his project. He will start by analyzing the feasibility of each of his ideas and choosing the one that appears to be the best. He will now begin to apply his IT skills to make the software for the market. This is what convergent thinking is about. Occasionally when he gets stuck, he may tune back to the free-flow mode and go back into a divergent thinking process to generate more ideas for a different stage of his software project.

As stated earlier, creativity is more linked to divergent thinking. But this does not mean that creative people never engage in a convergent thinking process. It merely means that those who only or always engage in the convergent thinking process have difficulties coming up with new ideas.

The bad news is that many school systems encourage us to be more convergent thinkers than divergent thinkers. We are trained from an early age to always base on already concluded criteria or standards to find solutions to problems. We have been made to believe that any given question calls for one right response. What we were taught in schools is not so different from what we experience in the workplace. We are always forced to stay in our restrained mode to find solutions for problems. We rely on standard practices and procedures. It prevents us from generating novel ideas because, to generate new ideas, we would need to engage in divergent thinking.

If we want to be creative, we need to give our brains the opportunities to be in a free-flowing mode and generate freely new ideas. It does not happen when we are always restricted to think in a certain way. We should be in a free-flowing mode when generating ideas, and in the restrained-mode when evaluating those ideas based on some structures, standards, and criteria.

Discover your mental abilities

We have discussed the relationship between intelligence and creativity. We have also looked at the different mental abilities and how they are linked to the creative potential. We have understood how we use our thinking capabilities to come up with creative ideas and products. However, the big question is still unanswered. How can you discover your mental abilities?

There are a lot of aptitude tests in the market that may help people know their mental abilities. It may be somehow daunting for you to know which of these can give you an accurate picture of your cognitive capabilities. My simple advice to you is to go through the following simple steps:

- Write your life story focusing on the things you

did in the past. Remember to also think outside of school and work environments. Start from when you were playing hide and seek with other children. Remember breaking and fixing some items. Remember telling stories to your friends, including those that you had just made up. Remember singing and dancing for your parents. Remember drawing flowers for your childhood girlfriend. Remember when you played football at school. Remember, Remember, and Remember!

- As you write your story, note those things you did, for which you often received compliments. Note those things you did, and you felt like you never struggled to do it. Note what other people have told you about what you did. Remember to note those things you dared doing, and you felt like it wasn't coming naturally.
- Write down things that you never tried before because you never had any chance and feel you may want to try.
- Open up for new experiences to re-do what you dared doing as a child, and you felt like it was coming naturally. Open up for new experiences to try new things.
- At this stage, we are talking about mental abilities, but not our motives or interests. Analyze the mental process you go through during the activity and not the emotional attachment you have towards the venture. Does it come naturally? Do ideas on how to do it flow in your head naturally? Does it feel like you are good at it?

The first step of this journey towards turning your creative potential into success has helped you assess your situation and understand why you may think there is nothing you can do to use your full creative potential.

The second step has convinced you that you may have what it takes to be creative in terms of mental abilities that are important to generate creative ideas and engage in creative production.

However, mental abilities explain only a part of who you are as a whole and unique person. It does not tell us much about the patterns of thought, feelings, and behaviors that make you unique, and which may influence how you put your mental abilities at work. The third step of this journey towards turning your creative potential into success is to understand your personality.

STEP 3

Understand Your Personality

You have made a step towards discovering your creative potential by acknowledging your mental capabilities. However, you recall some people told you that there are certain things you cannot do because of how you behave. They think you are too shy to express your ideas. They think you are too careless to follow through your work. They think you are too conventional to explore new opportunities. They believe you are short-tempered and not emotionally stable. They think you are this or that, and they tell you that you will not achieve success in life because of how you are. They intend to describe your personality and how it affects how you think, feel, and act.

Different people in different contexts often use the word personality, and it seems like many understand what it means. However, it has also been a debatable concept by psychologists. When we refer to somebody's personality, we usually refer to how he/she reacts to different situations similarly. It is also about how different people react to similar situations in different ways. We can tell whether or not the person likes to try new things. We can tell whether or not the person is organized and efficient. We can tell whether or not the person likes to socialize or call attention to him or herself. We can tell whether or not a person is compassionate and cooperative. We can tell whether or not the person can control his/her emotions, such as anger and anxiety. There are different theories on personality, but the one that has gained widespread acceptance among many psychologists is the Big Five Personality Traits. It is about five broad domains or dimensions of personality.

Personality is about the patterns of thought, feelings, and behaviors that make us unique. Many psychologists have studied personality and tried to understand factors that may contribute to it. Those from the psychoanalytic perspectives emphasize the fact that early childhood experiences affect our personality. They see a correlation between how we behave and our childhood experiences. On the other hand, those who analyze personality from the humanistic perspective emphasize free will and personal awareness. They suggest that we can influence how we think, feel, and behave based on our personal awareness and free will. Other psychologists focus on traits, based on which they categorize people's personalities. These psychologists suggest that some personality traits are inherent, and others are environmentally determined.

We can understand from the different theories that personality is influenced by both heritability and environmental factors. However, we can add to this that we, as individuals, can influence how we think, feel, and behave through our will and self-awareness. That's why we talk about learning behaviors such as empathetic listening, stress management, interpersonal skills, and other soft skills. It is because we are aware of the fact that we can influence how we think, feel, and behave.

So let's analyze the different personality traits and how they are linked to creativity or only to how we tap into our creative potential to generate creative ideas and products. While mental capabilities that we have discussed in step two are the 'what,' personality is the 'how' of the creativity equation.

Are you inventive and curious or consistent and cautious?

One of the personality traits is referred to as openness to experience. People who score high on this trait are curious and inventive. They are more imaginative, independent, and interested in variety. They like to break, make, or adapt to new things. People who score high on 'openness to experience' have more chances of using their creative potential. They like to seek new experiences, can come up with novel ideas, or seek to understand the linkages between ideas.

Those who score low on the trait of openness to experience are cautious, consistent, conventional, and traditional. They are more comfortable with familiar and traditional experiences.

For creative people, curiosity is just like play. They enjoy trying new experiences. They are curious to know how things can work differently, and the adventure of finding out is just fun to them.

I have had an opportunity to talk to some musicians in my country about the circumstances that led to some of their songs. It was interesting to hear that sometimes they see a lady passing by, then imagine where she is going and what shall happen when she gets there. They play with their imagination, and before you know it, they start singing that lady's story. The same applies to how I come up with my stories or poems. It's often from the imagination of what might have happened or could happen if a person with interesting characteristics had found him/herself in a given situation. Through writing, I satisfy my curiosity by coming up with hypotheses and testing them with a story.

One day, our daughter Bliss, when she was seven, told me that their teacher had told them something she was not convinced about. The question was, "why can't fish live out of water?" To me, it sounded astonishing; because I felt like at her age, she should already know. Then I asked her what the teacher had said. She replied that the teacher had said fish have gills instead of lungs and that gills take oxygen from water and not air. To me, that sounded like a complete answer. I asked my daughter why she wasn't convinced. She said that it should not be about lungs or gills because oxygen is the most important thing. The most important part of the story is that I told her she could do some more research on the internet to learn more about how fish breathe. She immediately said to me, "Mom, I know I can go to Google, but I do not want to do it that way. I want to go to a lake, get a fish out of the water, and see how it struggles to breathe." I was amazed by her thinking.

Creative people will want to see things, interact with them, fantasize on how they can work differently, serve other purposes, try them, play with their shape, weight, and height, move them, stop them, and have fun with those experiments. You will note that the interaction is not always with touch. It may be with all other senses.

Those who are consistent or cautious; on the other hand, are afraid to try new things. They find comfort in doing what they are familiar with. These are people who might say, "This is how I have done it for the last ten years." They value abiding by rules, policies, and standard procedures. When they would like to start some new ventures, they will only go for the well-proven sectors and industries. These people do not change jobs often, though they may not add much value to their organization's competitiveness.

It's indeed essential to be cautious, but it's also important to understand that the world keeps changing, and the more we are adaptive and open to new experiences, the better.

Are you efficient and organized or easygoing and careless?

It is about the personality trait of conscientiousness. People who score high on this trait are thorough, careful, or vigilant. They are hardworking and motivated to perform efficiently the tasks assigned to them. Conscientious people are organized, tidy, and efficient. This trait is very much linked to performance in schools and workplaces.

However, people with very high levels of conscientiousness may be workaholics, perfectionists, and less tolerant of mistakes.

On the other hand, people who score low on conscientiousness are easygoing, careless, and disorderly. They tend to be spontaneous and less goal-oriented and may act before they plan. Very low scores on this trait may lead to procrastination and less drive to achieve success.

Research has not found considerable significant correlations between the trait of conscientiousness and creativity. However, it is believed that conscientious people tend to be more successful in life. We understand that while the first trait we discussed of 'openness to experience' leads to imagination and generation of new ideas, engaging in the process to turn these ideas into new and useful products may require a certain level of conscientiousness.

We have already discussed the concepts of free-flow mode and restrained mode. When in free-flow mode, creative people are open to new experiences and curious to know how things can work differently or serve various purposes. They are curious to find out. They will then switch to the restrained mode to plan how they can engage in their experiments and organize their time and financial resources for their creative production.

However, when a person scores very high on conscientiousness, on the one hand, and very low on openness to experience, on the other, he/she may have difficulty to come up with new ideas, and in some cases, prevent new ideas from being implemented.

Think of a very organized and efficient manager who wants every task to be pre-planned before the implementation. If this manager is open to new experiences, all he/she will ask from team members is to think through their new ideas and suggest how these can be implemented. This manager shall help the team members compile plans or courses of action, identify and allocate resources to their project, schedule monitoring sessions to evaluate the courses of action, review plans, and re-strategize. On the other hand, a manager who scored high on conscientiousness and less open to new experiences may not adopt any new ideas. This is because he/she may want to be convinced that no mistakes shall be made, and no resources shall be wasted. In most cases, and, in reality, this assurance cannot be given. Since this manager is not open to trying the experience, he ends up saying no.

Let's take an example of an aspiring novelist, like me. She has a lot of imagination. She thinks that she can write novels that speak to people's everyday lives in her society. She will use her stories to talk about experiences people go through on this earth. She is a great storyteller. Whenever she is with her friends, she spontaneously tells stories, some real and others from her imagination. She decides she has to write her debut novel. When she starts writing, more inspiration continues to invade her thoughts, and she finds that exciting. She discovers she does not have ideas for only one novel, but many. She decides to work on five novels simultaneously. She spends a lot of time daydreaming about her stories, but sometimes she does not find time to write. She shall spend years writing her novels until she drops them unfinished. She had a very brilliant idea of writing five novels simultaneously. She has what it takes to do so. Why not? Why can't she write five novels simultaneously? Her only problem is that she cannot sit down and plan how to go about her writing. She cannot determine how much time she will need to spend on her writing every day. She is not able to decide on other resources she will need. Does she need a writing coach? Does she need an agent? Shall she self-publish her novels? Shall she go for traditional publishing? When does she intend to complete her books? What are the main characters in her stories? Where were the characters? What are the characters' objectives? What does she intend to achieve with her novels?

The difference between her and a novelist who combines imagination with conscientiousness is that the conscientious novelist, after coming up with the idea for a novel, he/she sits down to map his/her writing project. He/she identifies the resources he/she will need, spare some regular time for his/her writing, determine a tentative date when he/she will complete the first novel, then the second, till when he/she is done with the fifth.

From the examples above, we understand that although conscientiousness as a single personality trait does not correlate directly with creativity, it is a trait of successful creative people, who do not only have creative ideas, but also efficiently plan and implement their creative production, and bless the world with their creative or innovative products.

Having the mental abilities needed for creativity is one thing; being curious and inventive is another essential characteristic of creative people. However, for the creative person to achieve success in what he/she does, he/she needs to be organized and efficient.

I don't think I score very high on conscientiousness because I tend to be more easygoing than efficient. I like to take things easy. I sometimes procrastinate. It is not good. To mitigate it, I have given myself a structure. I have given myself a target of writing at least two thousand words a day. If not the book, it's a poem or a short story. For poetry, I like to use the notes on my phone. I write on the go, whenever I have inspiration for another stanza. On top of writing, I have another full-time job and a family with young kids that need me. To be successful everywhere, I need to be super organized. It's not so much about how much I do; it's about having time for everything, however little it might be. As a creative person, I need to have a work plan, draw a daily schedule, and set deadlines.

Are you outgoing and energetic or solitary and reserved?

The next personality trait is extroversion and introversion. People who score high on this trait, otherwise known as extroverts, tend to be energetic, talkative, assertive, and outgoing. On the other hand, those who score low are known as introverts and tend to be more reserved and solitary.

There is a common mistake of confusing introversion and shyness. Introverts are not necessarily shy. They can express themselves, but they like to be reserved and solitary.

There is a misconception that creative people are always extroverts. It is not true. Creative people can be either extroverted or introverted or, in some cases, ambivert; the middle point. The only difference between extroverts and introverts is how they choose to express their creativity as far as creativity is concerned. Extroverts enjoy human interaction, and they like to attract attention to them. They are rewarded by gratification from outside. Introverts, on the other hand, are motivated by interacting with their own mental life. They enjoy solitary activities.

Most creative extroverts enjoy activities that involve social gatherings and parties. Extroverts shall choose career paths that shall satisfy their need to interact with people. They enjoy working as politicians, evangelists, civil activists, singers, dancers, motivational speakers, TV show personalities, etc. They may be engaged in other career paths but shall continue to be motivated by the number of people they interact with and how much they can get their ideas known by many people. In today's society, having many followers on social media is one of the key motivators of extroverts.

Most introverts value more the inner rewards they get from engaging in an activity. For example, an introvert may write a film script. When the movie is out, he will enjoy seeing how the characters interact and how the film achieves its intended goals. Many introverts shall enjoy working as engineers, computer scientists, writers, painters, sculptors, etc. They can interact with other people, but like the moments they spend alone. It should be underlined that there is a difference between being introverted and antisocial.

As earlier said, the particularities of this personality trait, as far as creativity is concerned, is that both those who score high and those who score low on extraversion can engage in a creative process. The only difference is how they express their creativity and what motivates them as individuals. Another thing worth mentioning is that many people find themselves in the middle; like most other personality traits, some tend towards either extroversion or introversion. Many successful creative people enjoy interacting with other people, but they also like to get some time off to be alone.

I have never had to ask myself whether I am extroverted or introverted. All my friends would immediately tell me I'm extroverted. I like to express my ideas, and I don't care who is in the room or how many people are there. I enjoy interacting with people. When I was younger, you could never find me alone in a room. I was never solitary. However, In 1994, after the Genocide against the Tutsi, solitude became my best friend. I was 15 years old and did not quite understand what had happened to my family and my country. I had a lot to say but no words to express it. The only people who listened were my deceased father and brothers. I used to lock myself into a room to talk to them. I wrote them letters which I immediately tore. I asked them questions. I remember that I could be with other people and say goodbye to them because I wanted to go to my room to talk to my ghosts. Then, a few years later, I also discovered prayers. It did not stop me from talking to Papa and my brothers, but they had to share that precious time with God. I guess that's why, even today, you may conclude I like people's company if you see me at a party. Don't be surprised if the next time you invite me, I say no. My friends hate that about me. You never know when I want to be with people or when I want to be alone. So, I'm extroverted, but sometimes I enjoy solitary time. In my solitary time, I think, feel and write. When I'm with others, I observe, talk, and enjoy!

Are you friendly and cooperative or skeptical and detached?

It is about the 'agreeableness' personality trait. People who score high on this trait tend to trust and believe other people. In their social interactions, they are friendly and cooperative. On the other hand, those who score low on agreeableness tend to be skeptical about others' motives, and in their social interactions with other people, they tend to be detached.

Agreeable people tend to be passionate and like to help other people. They are empathetic to other people's needs and tend to be selfless in their relationships. On the other hand, less agreeable people tend to be selfish and insensitive to other people's opinions.

Are you friendly and cooperative or skeptical and detached? These are big words because they are both at the extremes of the agreeableness personality trait. Very high levels of agreeableness may lead to conformity and influence of choice. On the other hand, very low agreeableness levels may lead to cynicism, self-centeredness, and disconnection from society.

Successful people have moderate levels of agreeableness. They choose when to listen to other people's opinions and when to act based on their judgment. They decide when to cooperate with others and when to work as individuals. They choose how many hours they spend in a group and how many hours they spend alone. These people are unlikely to regret the effects of peer pressure. These people are likely to celebrate both group success and their success. These people are likely to appreciate both diversity of ideas and their uniqueness.

In the workplace, agreeable people are better team

players than the less agreeable people. They tend to appreciate other team members' contributions and help those team members who may need help. However, they tend to suffer the fact that, in some cases, other people do not recognize their individual contributions. On the other hand, less agreeable employees tend to contribute as individuals and celebrate their success. Those scored very low on agreeableness may be egotistical and warlike in a team.

Alice, my former colleague, was working on planning a big event for the organization. She was so excited. She had all sorts of ideas on how she would go about the task. She had done some research, set her goals, planned how she would design and decorate the event venue, designed the invitation cards, and outlined the event's flow. Alice had done a lot of thinking and planning for the event. It was so exciting for her to imagine a successful event. Then, one day Alice came to my office unhappy. She complained that the company's management had set up a team of people who would work with Alice on planning for the event. They had had their first meeting, during which some of Alice's ideas were rejected. Alice was frustrated. I was failing to understand why, because I expected her to be happy that the management had given her a team of people with whom to work. She said, "when you want a task to fail, you give it to a committee." In Alice's opinion, people do better as individuals and not as groups. She explained to me that it is not always evident that the group or committee adopts the very best ideas. There are so many factors that come into play. These factors include, for example, power dynamics in the group, and the fact that consensus means accommodating some views and compromising others. Alice thought that, in most cases, the aim for consensus dilutes the freshness of ideas and delays delivery.

It's prevalent to hear successful creative people telling stories of times when they had to make some radical decisions that were, in some cases, not accepted by some of their relatives or friends. I have already discussed the day my younger brother, an artist, announced that he was dropping out of school. If he had listened to us, he would probably have not achieved his dreams of being an artist, at least at that age. Did he need to drop out of school? Even today, some of us may have different opinions on that. But is he successful with what he is doing? None of us are doubtful about that. Would he have achieved the same success if he had combined his art and school? We cannot tell.

I never knew 'agreeableness' as a personality trait, would be a challenge to me because I thought of myself as a people-person, empathetic, and understanding. I had no idea the extent to which some people would want me to think and act like them, lest they withdraw their acceptance and approval. Yes, I knew they would criticize my work and tell me how substandard it could be. However, I didn't think they would want to push me to say what I didn't want to say or act the way I had not decided to do.

In the past, I had had experiences when I refused to listen to relatives or friends and made decisions they disapproved of. For example, when I decided to join another religious denomination, in which, a few years later, I realized I did not fit, my mother was not in agreement with me, but I did not listen. I also chose to ignore other people's opinions when I decided to specialize in Human Resources Management when family and friends advised me to select either Finance or accounting. The most significant decision I made without considering other people's opinions was my marriage. In all these experiences, the people who tried to advise me were relatives and friends, who remained by my side even after I had decided not to follow their guidance. Even when I left my former church, although some people cut contact, I maintained friendships with those who cared for me as a person, and not necessarily a believer.

The worst experience was after the publication of my debut novel, 'Hearts Among Ourselves'. Yes, the story I wrote is somehow unconventional, and I expected to receive both positive and negative feedback. That's okay. Interestingly, up to today, I have only received positive feedback from those who read the book, and these are members of the different groups that make up the Rwandan diversity. However, this positive feedback came with expectations, depending on what part of the story, one reader or the other liked. Like any other writer who tells stories to start a conversation, I used social media to interact with readers and potential readers, especially on the social issues addressed by the novel. I became more visible for both good and bad reasons.

Initially, I enjoyed the interaction with those who shared my opinions and those I disagreed with. I thought that's what Rwanda needed. A few months later, I realized that, in a polarized society like ours, people do not engage in discussions and debates to find common grounds. It was as if I was pulled left or right by those who did not care much about my feelings, experiences, and opinions, but who wanted to force me to adopt their understanding, use the same vocabulary they used, curse whoever they cursed, and praise whoever they praised.

In October 2018, I unfriended on Facebook a group of acquaintances, not because they were unkind people, but because they seemed worried that I was expanding my network to include people I should not mingle with. That would not be a big problem if they had not verbally abused me for having not subscribed to their divisive tendencies. I concluded, these people felt as if they owned me and did not want me to interact with all my compatriots, without any distinction.

In February 2020, I unfriended another group of acquaintances. Surprisingly, most of these were those the first group of people had warned me about my interaction with them. This group was mostly composed of compatriots I had connected with on social media after my debut novel was published. Once again, I did not unfriend them because they were evil. The challenge was that they, too, had expectations that I could not meet. They pulled me to their fights. They wanted me to serve their purposes, which somehow contracted mine. When I did not, they verbally abused me. When they attacked me on Facebook, I felt so bad because I concluded I had called it to myself.

Did I have to unfriend some of my compatriots on Facebook? No. Should creative people cut contacts with everybody who disagrees with their ideas? Not at all. I unfriended them simply because I was not emotionally prepared for the pressure. I unfriended them because some of them had crossed the line and started verbally abusing me. I unfriended them because I could not bear with their noise. I'm not advising you to do the same. I simply would like you to be aware of this challenge and learn that people interpret your work differently when you're creative. When you decide to express yourself, some people expect you to say something about almost everything, but when you say it your way, they are sometimes disappointed, and you might not know how they shall express their disappointment.

In this era of social media, people who score high on agreeableness judge their creative work's effectiveness by the number of people who follow them on social media, like what they post, positively comment on their ideas, and watch their videos, if any. However, these followers come with expectations, often divergent, and it's a challenge for the creative person to meet all of the audience's expectations. What happens is that the creative person chooses to either serve the purpose of a group that he/she thinks shall be loyal to him/her, at the stake of another group or other groups. This decision often leads to the loss of originality in what he/she does. If he/she does not want to lean to the demands of one group, but at the same time, does not want to hurt anybody's feelings, he/she ends up giving up on his/her creative contributions.

The reality is that some people have their agendas, and when you are creative, they want you to produce for them the tools they need to achieve their own goals. They don't necessarily say that to you. Maybe they don't even know that's what they are doing. They simply feel you're not helping their cause. It is even noticeable in a divided society like my native Rwanda, because of our history. As a Rwandan writer, I have to guard my independence of thought and originality of ideas. That's how I will be able to contribute to a better future for all Rwandans, without serving the interests of one group or the other.

We are all afraid of the unknown, and creativity means coming up with new ideas and objects. With the fear of the unknown, a lot of people will disapprove of your creative ideas. The level of connection you need, the level of trust you have in their judgment, the level of sensitivity you have to other people's opinions shall affect the evaluation of your ideas and your decision to pursue their implementation. If you score very highly on agreeableness, you will drop your creative ideas as long as other people disapprove of them. If you are less agreeable, you may not listen to the people who will want to contribute, not necessarily to your ideas' originality but their usefulness. If you are moderately agreeable, you shall listen to other people's opinions to only use their ideas to verify and evaluate your original ideas' effectiveness, but not to blindly do as they say and give up on your creative projects.

Are you sensitive and nervous or secure and confident?

Now, we are going to discuss the personality trait of neuroticism. People who score high on this trait tend to be characterized by irritability, bad temper, anxiety, nervousness, anger, envy, bitterness, and jealousy. These people tend to interpret ordinary situations as frightening and insignificant frustrations as extremely difficult. On the other hand, those who score low on neuroticism tend to be emotionally stable and adequately manage stress. Less neurotic people can control their emotions and temper. They usually feel more secure and confident than those who score high on neuroticism.

Let's look at some examples. Peter, Patrick, and John have been working for Company ABC for ten years. The CEO of company ABC has announced that they will lay off 50% of employees in the next two months. Peter is worried that he may be among those who would lose his job. He never saw it coming and does not have enough savings to rely on to provide for his family, should he be among those laid off. He is worried he may find himself in an uncertain situation.

On the other hand, Patrick is sure that there is no way he could be among the 50% of employees the company shall lay off. He recalls that he was praised among the best performers for all the ten years he has been working for the company. He knows that one of the managers told him that budget constraints might lead to abolishing his position. Still, Patrick believes that even if they abolish his job, the company shall give him another role because they cannot afford to lose the best performer.

Lastly, John is too worried and nervous. He cannot bear the news of the layoff. He thinks many people in the organization do not like him and may take the opportunity to get him dismissed.

Peter decides that although he is not sure whether or not he will be among those laid off, he should use the two months to get prepared. He thinks that he will lose nothing if he prepares for whatever the outcome of the layoff. He understands that he was not supposed to have spent all his savings. He decides to sell his fancy car and buy a cheaper model. He gains from that transaction $4,000 and decides to put this money in his savings account. He thinks that he will use the funds to start up a small home-based business, should he be laid off. It reduces some levels of his worry, but he spends a lot of time thinking about what kind of home-based business he shall venture into. Many ideas keep flowing in his head, and some of them, he thinks, are worth pursuing. He starts feeling that maybe if he is laid off, it will open up some opportunities to do what he would enjoy. He decides to start the home-based business as he waits for the outcome of the layoff exercise. He picks among his many ideas the business of producing cartoon videos and selling them downloadable from the website he designed.

For Patrick, since he is not worried about losing his job, he chooses to do nothing. He is sure that it would not be difficult for him to find another job, should he be laid off. But why would he even think like that? Who would decide to fire him?

John does not know what to do. He has no energy to continue working. He feels angry at the company's management. He feels like he has given his best to the company, and it would be unjust if he gets laid off. However, he is convinced he shall be among those to be laid off because his colleagues dislike him. He decides to confront the CEO, ask him if he is indeed among those that shall be laid off, and get more clarification about that layoff. He goes to the CEO's office for a conversation. The CEO explains the reasons for the layoff. One of the reasons for the layoff is that the company has not been making profits for some time, which has affected its capacity to sustain itself. John is furious to hear that. He works in the accounting unit and occasionally advised the company about its overheads, but the CEO never considered his pieces of advice. He angrily tells the CEO that it is his fault and that if he had not been that stupid, the company would not be having those difficulties. The CEO asks John to control his anger and use proper language. John says that there is no way he can hold his anger when he might lose his job. He makes noise in the CEO's office until other colleagues come and take him out. The CEO decides that John is not an employee to keep in the company and should be dismissed. He writes to the Human Resources unit to do the necessary. After receiving a request for an explanation, John is given a dismissal letter and loses his job.

Two months later, the company's management announces the layoff decisions. Both Peter and Patrick are among the employees fortunate to continue working for the company. The rumors are that even John was not on the list of those who were laid off. All three staff members, Peter, Patrick, and John, had nothing to worry about.

Three years later, Peter's business makes a monthly profit of $30,000, which is ten times his ABC Company salary. He decides to resign from ABC Company and focus on his business. Patrick is still with ABC Company on the same job, and his salary has been increased by 5%. He is now paid $3,150 per month. John has been getting some petty jobs but has not been able to secure a full-time job. He is indebted and depressed.

In this example, you can see how our level of neuroticism affects our decisions. We need to worry about our surroundings and circumstances enough to explore new ideas of making our situations better. It is what Peter did. Peter was moderately worried, but not too concerned and anxious to the extent of losing sight of the opportunities available in his surroundings. Patrick had no worries in life. His level of neuroticism was very low. He was happy with his status quo and did not see any reasons to change it. He does not have any urge to think about any potential opportunities he may grab to make tomorrow better than today. John has very high neuroticism levels to the extent of being consumed by worry, anxiety, and nervousness, and act in an uncontrolled way.

Even though neuroticism generally correlates negatively with creativity, I am aware that I don't score very low on this personality trait. I sometimes worry too much, and that's for me a two-edged sword. Sometimes, I see trouble where others don't. I'm sensitive to the words people choose to use when talking to me or others, how people treat me or others, and how they interact with one another. It somehow influences my creative work. When I feel pain or sadness, I often find refuge in writing. It feels as if I see through people's appearances and can share their pain and hurt. However, even though my worry contributes somehow to my writing, it does not serve me to be broken easily. I don't take lightly bad words, sarcasm, and anything that I may interpret as motivated by hate or inconsideration. As a creative person, I need to keep my level of worry only to what I need to create solutions instead of the worry that feeds my pessimism and leads me to give up. I have to protect myself from any emotional harm. That's why I sometimes decide to withdraw from some spaces and take time to deal with my own emotions. That's what John should have done instead of venting his anger to the company's CEO. As a writer, it's essential for me to take time to observe, be inspired, and create what to offer to the world. I do not want to recycle the rubbish the world throws to me. For example, I don't want my writing to be influenced by the insults and hate speech we often see on social media. I don't want my stories to be filled with only pessimism, but also optimism. I want to listen to good music and talk to best friends. I want to discover the beauty of our diversity and write stories that celebrate it. I want to write more about love and less about hate.

To conclude on this trait, creative people do not score highly on neuroticism. They are not too worried to the extent of giving up. However, they are not ignorant of the challenges and difficulties we all encounter in life, and that's what pushes them to come up with new ideas on how they can make things better. In addition to their desire to seek new experiences, creative people aim to change how things operate and make the world a better place. For example, when some of us may be worried about the effects of climate change, the creative person might be trying to find out new ways of preserving the environment. When people of Rwanda may be worried about the divisions that led to the tragic events in our history, the creative people might be thinking about innovative tools to engage and reunite our torn society.

Understand your personality traits

You now understand that you are more creative when

you have the personality trait of openness to experience, expressed through being curious and inventive. You have also understood the importance of being moderately conscientious, organized, and efficient, but not too conscientious to the extent of being a perfectionist who may not dare try new things due to fear of making mistakes. You have understood that being either extrovert or introvert does not influence your ability to be creative, but, in some cases, how you choose to express your creativity. You have understood that as much as it's essential to be friendly and sensitive to other people's opinions, it should not be to the extent of searching for conformity and approval, with the risk of losing your uniqueness and individuality. You have understood that, as a creative person, the level of your worry should be what leads to the decision to search for solutions and take measures to overcome challenges, but not the anxiety that leads you to give up.

After these three steps that helped you analyze your situation, discover your mental abilities and understand your personality, the only other question you would like to answer is if you want to turn your creative potential into success. You are right; not all people who have the mental abilities and the personality traits necessary for creativity come up with creative ideas and objects. Some motives push you to use this potential and generate creative ideas and produce innovative products. You are now going to make the fourth step, which is about knowing your motivation factors.

STEP 4

Know Your Motivation Factors

To be creative, we need to be good at what we do. We need to have the ability to think and reason logically and the ability to apply the acquired knowledge for the production of novel ideas and objects. We need the right mental capabilities, and that's what I call the "what" of the equation. Our creativity goes through a process from the generation of ideas to the production of novel objects. Our patterns of thought, behavior, and feelings determine our success in this creative process. That's the role of personality, and what I call the "how" of the equation. To go through a creative process and pursue its success to the end, we need to be motivated, and motivation is what I call the "why" of the equation. Motivation multiplies the efforts of both the mental abilities and personality.

Motivation is defined as the reason for behaving or acting in a particular way. We do what we do because we either like it or have to fulfill a purpose or satisfy a need. Sometimes we are conscious of the motives that lead to our behaviors and actions. Some other times we are unconscious of why we do what we do. Motivation may be innately generated, known as intrinsic motivation, or be conditioned; extrinsic motivation. It's essential to understand why we do what we do, so that we may determine how to do it.

I will classify motivation factors into three types: passionate interest, personal drive, and need satisfaction. You will understand that it is difficult to put a clear cut between the three because one leads to the other in most cases.

Passionate interest

Passion or interest is the type of motivation some people may find difficult to explain. How would you explain your love for birds? Why do you spend money to go to places only to see birds? You are fascinated by their colors, their ability to fly, their way of living, and you just want to know more about birds. How would you explain it to someone who does not have the same passion for birds? Some other people have a passion for colors. They are fascinated by how more shades of color than we can imagine are in our surroundings. They spend their time mixing colors and enjoying the shades they come up with from combining two or more primary colors, then two or more secondary colors, then two or more tertiary colors, then another level, and another level. They find it exciting and passionately enjoy the experience.

We all have different passionate interests, and in most cases, we cannot explain why we have a passion for this or that. It catches our attention. We like to think about it, to explore it, and to discover more about it. If you ask me why I love writing, I may probably fail to tell you why. I write because I enjoy languages and their music. I like the way it keeps me busy. It's like a sport for my brain. It's the music I dance in silence without having to be on the dancefloor.

How do we develop our interests? We may have developed particular interests from our childhood experiences, or later in our teenagerhood or adulthood. Although, in my childhood, I was exposed more to reading than writing, when I was a teenager, after the death of my father and brothers, writing became my refuge, the solace place where I met and chatted with my deceased loved ones. I was born in a landlocked country. My neighborhood was not close to any of the lakes in the region. Growing up, I did not interact with water so much. That probably explains why I did not develop an interest in surfing or fishing like those who grew up near beaches. We develop interests over time from the interaction with our surroundings through our senses. It may be the things we like to touch, those we love to see, those we prefer to hear, those we love to smell, those we enjoy to taste, or even those that we like to interact with through our intuition. So how do you develop an interest? You develop an interest or disinterest by trying out things.

Most of us may not want to develop an interest in new things. However, they might find it useful to discover what they have already developed an interest in and how this might be a good start for their creative endeavors.

If you would like to realize your interests, the best start should be to think about what makes you happy and put a smile on your face. Are you most pleased when singing, dancing, playing soccer, hiking, mountaineering, fishing, or breaking some machines? Are you a natural news reporter? How do you feel when you are cooking? Do you feel like it's a hobby or a house chore? Are you fascinated by the way technology changes people's lives and enjoy being part of that phenomenon?

It is entertaining to notice how some people are news reporters without necessarily working for any media? Many amateur cooks enjoy cooking more than professional chefs. How many singers who never intend to earn their living from singing? How about writers who list no single publication on their resumes? If you would like to know the interests many people have and how these can be turned into creative products, go to social media. It will be fascinating to see how many people enjoy cracking jokes without being credited as comedians. It will be interesting to see how many people like to report news on social media. I have not forgotten those who seem to have great ideas on ending poverty in Africa without being affiliated with the organizations working for that cause.

Look into your life and find out the things you are interested in. Probably you call them hobbies, or you do it just to have fun.

Do you think you have no specific interests? The good news is that there are some tips you may apply to discover your interests:

- Get out of your daily routine and be exposed to new experiences. Go for a different activity; playing golf, football, basketball or any other sport activity, playing guitar or piano, or just singing, joining a cooking club, learning a new language, gardening, etc. One activity at a time!
- Do not fake your interest. Go with the genuine

awareness that you do not know much about the activity and that you are not sure that you will end up liking it.
- If you go there once and it feels like you do not want to go back for the second time, stop going and pack it for another time when you will feel like trying again.
- If you go there and you want to go back, go.
- After trying the activity several times, evaluate your clues, and decide if you are interested in the activity.
- If you are not interested in the activity, drop it and go for another one.
- If you are interested in the activity, you will start wanting to know more about it, and later on, before you know it, it will have become a hobby you are passionate about.
- You have found a hobby and not a niche. Keep open to new experiences. Life has a lot of surprises!

What do our interests have to do with creativity and success? Whenever I get a chance to talk to some creative and successful people in their careers, most of them tell me similar stories. They all started with the things they liked to do in their childhood, or those they tried later and developed a passion for. Then, they move on to tell me how, when the opportunity to do what they liked presented itself to them, they immediately grabbed it. These are not only soccer players, musicians, top models, and artists. The list includes those who liked to break and make cars and machines and those who enjoyed reading, writing, and telling stories. It includes those who aspired to be politicians and those who aspired to be humanitarians. It includes successful people from all walks of life.

What are the steps for turning your passionate interest into your successful profession? You like it, and probably you are also good at it. Below are the steps you may take to turn your interest into a successful profession:

- Acquire more knowledge and skills in the area. My mother always had an interest in flowers, but she knew just enough about flowers. The day she decided to do gardening for a living, that's the time we saw her with reading glasses and books on gardening in her hands. That's the time I started seeing people coming home to teach her more about gardening. For some activities, you may need to enroll in a formal school. Yes, you may be a singer, but not a professional singer. Yes, you may be an actor, but not a professional actor. You may be a writer, but you need to acquire more creative writing skills. Yes, you may be a good evangelist, but you need to learn theology. I do not know how you will learn and how much you need to learn. All I know is that you need to take your hobby from the amateur to the professional level, which shall not happen over time.
- Find coaches and mentors in your area of interest. These are people that have gone through the ups and downs of what you want to do. Listen to their insights. Observe their behavior. Ask them questions. Make sure they are the channels through which you continue to get up-to-date

information on the hobby you are turning into a profession.
- Third, practice, practice, and practice. In French, they say "c'est *en forgeant qu'on devient forgeron*." In English, they say, "practice makes perfect." The best soccer players are those who did not only like to play soccer but who used to wake up early in the morning to play soccer every day. The same applies to all of us. A writer writes, a singer sings, a cook cooks, and a designer designs.
- Fourth, produce and sell. We will discuss this in detail when we reach the step on creative production. Whatever you choose to do as a creative person, you have to get into a workshop, produce your innovative products, package them, and distribute them. The same applies to both services and goods that you will need to distribute. Artists shall go to their studios; soccer players shall go to the stadium; writers shall write their manuscripts; businesspeople shall go to their shops; politicians shall gather in their political parties and parliament to do politics.

My piece of advice to parents:

We have already discussed how parents and schools should give children and young people opportunities to discover and develop their mental abilities. The same applies to interest. I advise parents to give their children opportunities to try out different hobbies and hopefully develop interests in various skills. It will come handy to them when they will be adults. By exposing children to different opportunities, you give them the chance to know themselves better; understand what they like and what they do not like; change it, and go back to it later; until the day, they shall choose to focus on some activities.

For some parents, instead of giving children opportunities to discover their interests, they push them towards what the parents like. If you take your child to a choir, but he/she comes back home saying that he/she does not want to go back, do not force him/her. The same applies to his/her music lessons or his/her swimming sessions. The beauty with children is that they will only drop it if you make it too formal and not playful. If you keep it fun, they will only quit when it's indeed not their thing. It takes some time before a child will start saying that she goes to school to study. Most children shall tell you that they go to school to play with their friends. The earlier we make learning fun, the better our children shall freely discover their abilities and interests and enjoy developing them.

I have seen people pursuing their passionate interests without expectation of achieving any other objectives in the future. Why would you even go the extra mile to find your interests? Why would you need to discover and develop your mental abilities? Why would you need to understand your personality and how you can build on your strengths to do best whatever you do? The simple reason is that you probably need to accomplish something in life. That takes us to discuss another critical motivation factor: personal drive.

Personal drive

Personal drive is an internal strong desire to accomplish

a purpose. It is what pushes you to put at use your mental abilities, adopt behaviors that nurture your creativity, find your passionate interests, and invest effort and time in making sure that you become who you aspire to be. Whatever the circumstances of your life, you have that force that pushes you to wake up every morning and embrace a new day with the determination to do better than the day before. Personal drive is that energy or that force that pushes you to aim for higher achievements and to pursue success in whatever you do. You may consciously know what it is, or unconsciously feel it.

Do you want to achieve success in your life? Most of us would answer yes to this question. But the question is: What do we understand by success? Does it mean climbing the corporate ladders to the highest? Does it mean making more money and becoming a billionaire? Does it mean becoming famous and popular? Does it mean gaining more power and respect in society? Does it mean changing the world or part of the world in one way or the other? What do you understand by success?

Let me ask you another question? When you read Forbes (if you ever do), which of the following lists is more appealing to you?

- World's Top 20 CEOs;
- World's billionaires;
- World's most powerful people;
- The celebrity 100 (world's celebrities);
- None of these. You would prefer the list that includes Mother Teresa;
- None of these. You would prefer the list that includes Nelson Mandela, Martin Luther King, Jr. or Mahatma Gandhi;

- Or you're like me; you probably prefer the list that includes names like Toni Morrison, Wole Soyinka, Maya Angelou, and Nadine Gordimer.

Another question: If you were given an opportunity to choose an inspiring person to share dinner with, would you choose the most prominent corporation's CEO? Would you choose the top self-made billionaire? Would you choose the most famous celebrity? Would you pick the president of the most powerful country in the world? Would you prefer the political revolutionist, who changed his/her country's realities? Would you choose to be with a professor from one of the top universities in the world? Would you prefer to be with the person whose humanitarian actions changed the lives of many? The list can go on. Who do you consider successful?

The conventional definition of success is the accomplishment of an aim or purpose. Personal drive, as earlier defined, it the strong internal desire to accomplish a purpose. Does this mean that you cannot talk of success when you did not have a purpose? Yes. Does it mean that you cannot speak of success when you did nothing to achieve that purpose? Yes. Does it mean that you cannot talk of success when you are not satisfied with how you achieved your purpose? Yes.

I still have a few more questions for you:

- If you were to change a thing in the world, what would that be?
- If you were told the exact day and time you will

die, what life goal would you want to have accomplished before death?
- If you were meant to write down the speech somebody shall make about you at your funeral, what would you want it to include?

As stated earlier, some people unconsciously answer these questions every day and work to make them their realities. Some other people have taken time to consciously think about these questions and define their purpose in life. Whatever group you belong to, there is that strong desire in you to accomplish a purpose, and that's what I call your personal drive.

Is it essential to discover your personal drive? Yes, it is. The sooner you discover your personal drive, the earlier you will decide to direct your actions towards turning your creative potential into success. When I talk about this, many people argue that it's impossible to think about a life purpose when you have immediate needs that need to be satisfied. That takes us to the third type of motivation.

Need satisfaction

While a passionate interest is about what you enjoy doing, a personal drive is about the goals you want to achieve when you do whatever you do. The third motivation factor is about the needs you want to satisfy.

A need can be defined as a lack of something necessary for you to live a healthy life. But what do we mean by a healthy life? It's about your wellbeing. We are healthy only when all the pillars of our life are in good shape. These are: physical, mental, emotional, economic, and spiritual. When a need is unsatisfied, your health is at stake. You satisfy your need to live a healthy life. Need satisfaction as a motivation factor, unlike passionate interest and personal drive, is about our daily survival.

Two need theories have gained considerable acceptance from scholars. The first one is the theory known as Maslow's hierarchy of needs, invented by Abraham Maslow. The second one is the Three Needs Theory by David C. McClelland.

According to Abraham Maslow, needs follow a particular hierarchy. Physiological needs have to be satisfied before a person thinks about his safety needs. After safety needs are satisfied, the person can start feeling the need for love and belonging. When this is met, then the person worries about his/her need for self-esteem, and lastly, his/her need for self-actualization. Although many psychologists support Maslow's theory on the hierarchy of needs, other psychologists argue that there is no hierarchy of needs.

David C. McClelland grouped needs into three types: the need for achievement, the need for affiliation, and the need for power. Those with a high need for achievement feel an individual desire for a significant accomplishment. Those with a more pressuring need for affiliation feel a sense of social involvement and belonging within a social group. Those with a high need for power are satisfied by influencing their surroundings.

My understanding is that whether we are talking of a hierarchy or categorization, we all have different needs as people and at the same time. However, some needs may be more pressuring than others. For example, although the person shall continue to feel the need for safety or self-esteem, when urged by the physiological needs, he/she will work to satisfy those first. However, that does not eliminate his/her needs for safety, love, belonging, self-esteem, and self-actualization. In the same line, some people may feel that the need for affiliation is more pressuring than other needs depending on their personal experiences. The same applies to the need for power or the need for achievement.

Need satisfaction is one of the motivation factors that I always find difficult to explain. In my opinion, although necessary to all of us, it is self-centered and momentary. It is about a person's wellbeing and survival. It is about calming down the physical or psychological pressure by doing something to feel better. When I am thirsty, I drink water. When I am hungry, I eat food. When I am not safe, I seek protection. When I am lonely, I look for the company of other people. When I am disrespected, I impose respect. When I feel modest, I need to do great things and self-actualize.

As I stated before, it's somehow difficult to get a clear cut between a personal drive and a need. However, if we evaluate what we do and why we do it, we can tell whether we are driven by a need, a purpose, or do it simply because we enjoy it. For example, a person may sing because he/she enjoys singing (passionate interest). He/she may also want to communicate an important message and choose singing as the channel (personal drive). He/she may also decide to sing because he/she believes it's one of the surest ways to earn a living, feed him/herself, pay for shelter, and satisfy other needs (Need satisfaction). The urge to satisfy a need may push a person to generate creative ideas and produce innovative products. However, for the creative production to sustain, the person might need another long-term reason to do what he/she does.

What motivates you?
After understanding your mental abilities and personality traits, you have gone through defining your motivation factors and how they affect your creativity. You now understand the importance of doing what you enjoy doing or have a passion for. You also recognize that you should not ignore the strong desire to achieve what you want to achieve or serve a particular purpose. You also understand that, sometimes, you do what you do only to satisfy a need.

Making this fourth step to know your motivation factors has awakened the urge to turn your creative potential into success. You now understand why you have to turn your creative potential into success. Why was this discussed in Part I of this guide? It's because motivation completes the equation of creative potential. It is the element that multiplies the sum of mental abilities and personality traits. Without motivation, you may not take further steps towards turning your creative potential into success. So, in conclusion, what did we learn about your creative potential in these first four steps?

End of Part I - Your creative potential
You were born with intelligence, the ability to think and reason logically and abstractly, acquire the knowledge,

and apply it in your everyday life. You continue to develop your intelligence to gain more knowledge, acquire new skills, and learn from new experiences. Your level of intelligence constitutes the ability to acquire and apply knowledge, skills, and experience. You have different mental abilities, and you have been able to discover what you are good at.

You have also realized you are a person with unique patterns of thoughts, feelings, and behaviors. You understand why you think, feel, behave how you do, and how it affects your creative potential. You're aware of your personality traits and how they correlate with your ability to generate creative ideas and produce innovative products.

Finally, you have discovered you have unique interests, and nobody and nothing shall stop you from doing what you love. You will excel not only in doing what you are good at but also in what you enjoy doing. You also understand that there is a purpose you want to accomplish, and are determined to put your creative potential at work, to fulfill this purpose. Like any other human being, you have needs. These will not hold you back. As you satisfy them, you will be taking steps towards accomplishing your purpose, and at the same time, doing what you are good at and what you have a passion for. Now you are ready to start moving, which leads us to Part II of this book, about entering the creativity workshops to embark on creative production.

PART II

CREATIVITY WORKSHOP

STEP 5

Define Your Life Purpose and Set Your Goals

Bliss, our daughter, got her first national passport in 2009, but it was only in 2014, five years later, that she used it. That was not because she did not have money to buy an air ticket because Dad and Mom could pay for it. It was not because she could not get a visa; she had never applied for one. The only reason she was not using her passport was that she had not figured out where to go, why, how, and what to do after getting there.

A lot of people are like Bliss. They have their passports to success but have never used it. They have an idea of what success may look like, but they do not know where it is. They do not get why they should take the journey to success. They do not know how they can get to success. They have not yet decided when they will go to success. The worst of all, most of them have not even figured out they have a passport to success.

When I was in school, I had what it took to complete my studies and obtain the highest degree. My parents and teachers had convinced me that formal education was my passport to success. I was always among the best students of my generation, which made me confident that the future would be bright. I studied, studied, and studied until that one day when I had to explain why I wanted to continue studying. On that day, I discussed with my husband my plan to go back to Europe to pursue a Ph.D. programme at a British University. The potential thesis supervisor had accepted my research proposal. I was looking forward to being a Ph.D. candidate, and later earn the title of 'Doctor.' My research proposal was about 'Creativity Killers in Africa'.

One day, my husband asked me an intelligent question to which, I think, I responded thoughtlessly. He asked me what I wanted to achieve with a Ph.D. I talked about the fact I always wanted to get a Ph.D., and that I was convinced it would lead me somewhere far in my career, even though I could not say where and how. I had a master's degree, and according to my husband, I would only need a Ph.D. if I wanted to pursue an academic career. No, I did not want to go into academia. I wanted to earn a Ph.D. My husband challenged me with examples of successful people in their careers, without a degree or with just a first degree. He reminded me that I did not have only a degree, but two degrees. He suggested that I should first evaluate what I used those degrees for. The conversation was taking a route I did not like. I said a lot, but it felt like I was saying nothing. I did not have an answer to his question. What was I going to do with a Ph.D.? I was going to be called Dr. Umwagarwa. I was going to add a few letters in front of or after my names. I was going to be respected more in the society. When I was younger, my parents had told me that I was intelligent and intelligent people study up to the Ph.D. level, right? Couldn't my husband understand that? I wondered. I decided to conclude the conversation, and I said: "Honey, if you love me, please let me go for the Ph.D. programme. I agree with you that it may not guarantee promotion in my career. It may not guarantee that, as a family, we shall be richer or wealthier. Just think about it as giving a gift to me. It has always been my dream to get the highest degree since I was little. If I don't do it, I will always feel like I never completed my studies."

Do you want to know what happened after? He approved the idea of just letting me go as a way of giving me a gift. Then we both waited for the response from the university. As we were waiting, I got an exciting job offer in an international organization. I decided to accept it, knowing that I would resign the day I would receive my admission letter to the Ph.D. programme. On my second day on the job, I received an email from the university, and it had an attachment. It was an admission letter. On the one hand, I looked at my job appointment letter and my admission letter on the other. I looked at them again, I read both of them, and then I made a decision. I wrote an email to the university that I was deferring the admission to the following year. Ten years later, I have not yet enrolled in a Ph.D. programme. I still want to, and I'm sure I will. Otherwise, if I don't earn a Ph.D. I shall have failed to turn into a reality one of my most important childhood dreams.

Why did it seem difficult for me to choose between pursuing Ph.D. studies and staying on that new job? My parents, teachers, and mentors always told me that formal education is a sure passport to success, and I still believe them. However, I have realized there is a lot they never told me. I wished they had told me what success meant, why I should pursue it, and how I would know I have achieved it. In the first part of this book, we discussed your creative potential, which I believe to be your passport to success. You have the mental abilities you need to acquire and apply knowledge, develop skills, and learn from experience. You are aware of your personality and understand why you think, feel, and behave the way you do. You have now decided to start a journey to success. You would like to know what milestones you should go through to get to success. You wonder what shall tell you that you are on the right track. The fifth step of the journey to turn your creative potential into success is defining your purpose and setting your goals.

Understanding your purpose and goals

I always wondered why a lot of people liked to watch soccer. What's interesting about looking at 22 people running after a ball for 90 minutes? When I was younger, I played soccer at school and felt good to play with boys when other girls could not dare to play soccer. It changed when I was a teen and started feeling more girly. Since then, I do not play, but occasionally watch soccer games to keep my husband company. Soccer is one of the most popular games. You may wonder why people fill up a stadium to watch soccer. The simple reason is that many of us relate somehow to the rules of that game or similar games such as basketball or handball. It's about scoring goals, and the more goals a team scores, the higher the chances of winning the game. However, to win a cup or a championship, a team would need to win many games. We can see the similarities between the soccer game rules and how we live and pursue success in our lives.

In life, we all have a purpose we want to fulfill. We want to win the cup of a successful life before death shall knock on our door. Some of us have been kicking the ball for so many years. However, all we do is moving from the east corner of the playground to the west corner, or from the south corner of the playground to the north. We enjoy the game and have managed to keep the ball with us for the most extended periods. When the ball is taken from us, we fight to get it back. Some of us have received yellow cards, but fortunately, we have not yet received a red card. We have been running for so long, and we are afraid that the referee may rule that the game is over before we score a goal.

A goal is defined as the end toward which effort is directed. If you want to win, you should direct the efforts you make every minute of your life towards a specific goal. You do not, however, need to have one goal in life. That's where a goal differs from a purpose. Many goals may be linked to one purpose. Goals and objectives are the exact measurable steps you will make towards accomplishing your purpose.

How to set goals

Have you ever planned a long trip? The first thing you determined was your destination. The second thing you ascertained was the length of your journey; the number of kilometers between your departure point and your destination point. The third thing you determined was the cost of getting there, and lastly, how long it would take you to get there. These are the same questions you should answer whenever you set your life goals. Your goal should be as specific and straightforward as possible. It should be defined so that it's easy to measure how far you are towards achieving it. A goal should take you to an end that is possible to reach. More importantly, the goals you set in your life should be relevant to the purpose you would like to fulfill in life, and finally, you should link all your goals to a timeframe. That is known as setting SMART goals, i.e., Specific, Measurable, Achievable, Relevant, and Time-bound goals.

Your goals should not only be SMART but balanced as well. Many people fail to meet their goals, not because the goals were not smart, but because they were not balanced. If you would like to serve a bigger purpose in life, your goals should be related to your life's pillars. If the goal is typically personal and about you living a happy and wealthy life, make sure it speaks to each of your life's five pillars, i.e., Intellectual, Physical, Emotional, Economic, and Spiritual. If the goal is about your contribution to the world we live in, make sure you keep it balanced as longer self-realization, social connectedness, and social responsibility aims are concerned.

Whenever you set your goals, you should determine your success indicators. What shall tell you that you have achieved your goals? These might be:

- Actionable: What shall you do?
- Quantitative: How many? How much?
- Directional: What improvement do you intend to make? What trend shall it take?
- Practical: How does it affect other aspects of your

life? What impact shall it have on your family? In your community? On society?
- Financial: How much shall it cost you? How much savings shall you gain? How much shall you make?

Defining your life purpose and setting your goals

As already discussed, I experienced tragic periods in my life. In 1994, my father, brothers, and other family members were killed by our compatriots. The experience changed the way I viewed the world. I became more concerned with the issues and realities that took away my loved ones. I may not go into details of the painful journey that took me so many years before I came to the conclusion that my biggest enemies are not any individuals or groups of people, but hatred and violence. Since that realization, I have always wondered how I can contribute to building a world where no other child shall lose a father, mother, or sibling due to hate or violence. A world in which no other girl shall experience the same abuses I experienced during my teenagerhood.

My life purpose may be defined as: Convincing my compatriots in particular, and world citizens, in general, that love, peace, and respect for diversity, should be our most important virtues. All other issues we continue to debate about shall be resolved, the day we shall aim at love and peace for all.

How shall I fulfill this purpose, and what shall tell me I am on the right track? As you can see, I aim to start a conversation, and if successful, convince those who shall engage with me in that conversation. That's why I chose to use both written and spoken words. That's why I write books, stories, and poems. That's why in addition to written materials, I produce audio and videos for both my stories and poems. That's one of the reasons I use social media and all other channels of communication.

To make the journey simpler and break it into specific steps, I have set both short-term and long-term goals. I try to make my goals as smart and balanced as possible. I may not discuss all my goals, which I frequently revisit and realign to new realities and circumstances. However, I believe you understand that my goals are about:

- The topics I address in my writing and the stories I tell. I aim at tackling all the issues linked somehow to the abstracts of hate and violence.
- The written and spoken materials I produce, books, short stories, poems, and others;
- The number of people I engage with, those who read my books, stories, or poetry, and the feedback I receive from those people.
- The ultimate goals may be about society's tangible changes, such as condemning hate and violence and promoting love and peace for all as virtues we should all embrace.

I believe I make my goals specific, measurable, achievable, relevant, and time-bound. However, the biggest challenge for me has been to keep my goals balanced, without appearing as if I'm doing less than what I should do. For example, I think about how whatever I do affects other pillars of my life, physical, emotional, intellectual, economic, and spiritual. I also have to think about my social connectedness and social responsibility. I might probably need to write a full book to discuss in detail how it has been challenging to me, not because my goals are not balanced, but because we live in a world that does not recognize the fullness of who we are. I want to succeed not only as a writer but also as a wife, mother, sister, friend, compatriot, and world citizen. I should always consider how my decisions may affect my loved ones' emotional and physical wellbeing. I do not want to solve some problems by creating others.

On the page where we discussed the personality trait of agreeableness, I have already told you how I have had to guard my emotional wellbeing and my social connectedness by, unfortunately, cutting contact with some friends on social media. I always wonder how to express love to haters without being intoxicated by their hate. Many people talk about love and peace only when directed to them or their groups. When you express love to those, they call their enemies, their definition of love changes. They feel offended simply because you are expressing love for others. It irritates them even though the intention was not to hurt them. Some other times, people get offended when you tell your truth about some social issues, maybe because they don't realize that love does not necessarily mean agreement. Balancing my self-realization, social connectedness, and social responsibility has been challenging, but I believe, one day, I will find the right balance.

To conclude on this
The first four steps you have made in this journey have

led to the realization that you have creative potential that you may turn into success. You now understand that your creative potential is your passport to success. In this fifth step, I believe you have defined what success means to you. What purpose do you want to fulfill, and what specific short-term and long-term goals shall you achieve on the journey to fulfilling your purpose? What you need to do now is drawing your strategies to achieve these goals, and that takes us to the sixth step.

STEP 6

Draw Your Strategies

A strategy is a pattern of decisions and actions directed towards achieving your goals. Now that you have defined your ultimate, long-term, and short-term goals, the next step is to draw your strategies. You understand that in steps 1, 2. 3, and 4 of this guide, we were trying to determine where you are today. In step 5, I have helped you decide where you want to be tomorrow, and beyond, by defining your life purpose and setting your goals. In step 6, we will discuss the pattern of decisions you shall make and the actions you shall take to pursue your life purpose and achieve your goals.

Let's go back to the example of my creative writing journey. I have already defined my life purpose and set my ultimate, long-term, and short-term goals. However, I have not discussed the strategies I shall devise to achieve these goals. In this step, I will take you through the four important ones: 1) Formulating a unique personal message, 2) creating a personal brand, 3) Communication and networking, and finally, 4) managing resources and finances.

It does not matter if you're employed and receive a monthly salary, an entrepreneur or self-employed, an artist, or any other way you would like to be referred to. We all need to devise strategies to achieve our personal and professional goals and fulfill our life purpose.

When you decide to travel, you do not only determine where to go and when to get there, you also strategize on how to get there. You know that traveling from East Africa to North America by walking may seem nearly impossible. You know that going by road may take many days and weeks, if not months, and you would probably need to consider taking a ferry to cross the sea or an airplane to fly. You think that traveling by air may be feasible, but you may miss the experience of exploring the world and its environment on the ground. Whatever decision you shall make in terms of how to get there, by foot, road, sea, or air, you will need to also make decisions on all those other factors that shall contribute to a successful and safe trip from East Africa to North America. That's the same thing you do when you devise the strategies to achieve your goals and accomplish your life purpose.

Essential elements of a strategy

Your life purpose and goals should be taken into consideration when devising your strategies. Whatever decision you make should not compromise your life purpose. I have realized that most successful musicians, artists, engineers, architects, computer scientists, physicians, managers, politicians, and other people in any profession, defined their unique personal message as the first element of their strategy. It guides everything they say or do. After determining their unique personal messages, these people make sure they transmit this message in all their interactions with the world, creating a personal brand they are always associated with. That's about the second element of their strategy: Brand and branding. Successful people seek and link up with not only like-minded people but everybody who can contribute in one way or the other to their success. That's networking, which is about leveraging interactions with other people; potential clients, sponsors, mentors, and everybody who might contribute to their success with his/her ideas, advice, guidance, skills, inspiration, etc. Last but not least, successful people strategize on what to invest in and how to manage effectively their resources and finances.

In strategizing your creative journey, you should think about the following:

- A unique Personal Message;
- Brand and Branding;
- People and Network; and
- Resources and Finances.

Let's start by looking at the first one: Unique Personal Message.

Unique personal message

It's is about defining your value proposition and making sure that whatever you do communicates this value proposition. It does not matter if you are employed for a salary or self-employed; we all need to define our unique personal message. It's about how you want to be understood by society regarding the contributions you propose to make. A unique message shall help you stay focused, connect with those who share your vision or philosophy or are affected by the social issues you aim to address. It should guide all other decisions you shall make. Your words and deeds should also communicate this message. It should guide your choice of relationships and the networks you connect to. It should be taken into account in all decisions you make about resources and finances.

Think about entrepreneurs like Steve Jobs, musicians like Bob Marley, television personalities like Oprah Winfrey, and politicians and revolutionaries like Nelson Mandela. You can surely tell what their unique personal messages are/were. Think about those in your country or region.

In my country, we have different musicians. If I only picked two, James and Joshua. They are both in the same music industry, but their unique personal messages seem different. James decided to address his message about love and relationships, and target those who believe in love. On the other hand, Joshua chose to convey hope to young people who struggle in life. He sings about their misery, but also the choices they make for survival. He communicates ambition and courage, and the fact that no obstacles shall stop a person who is ambitious and courageous. Imagine a storyline in the media that James had abused his girlfriend, or that Joshua had given up on life. Everyone would say that they do not practice what they preach. Are they preachers? No, they are just musicians.

Do I mean that you should only communicate one message? It depends on whether you decided to differentiate or to diversify your services. However, whatever way you choose, make sure that your different messages are in line with each other, and they all contribute to the fulfillment of your life purpose. Your communications and behaviors should not contradict each other.

Nowadays, there are so many ways individuals interact with the world, and believe me; however way you will try to avoid it; your words and behaviors convey a message. I bet you want to have control of what you communicate. Many people have professional websites, blogs, and social media platforms, and all they do is just sending information. I advise you to decide what it is you want to communicate. I do not mean that you should choose one topic to discuss. No. People will not feel you are genuine if you do that. I advise you to decide a line of your message and make sure all your communications help convey that message.

Think about someone who has decided to be an activist for human rights, and imagine, when he/she would say something against one group of people, maybe because of his/her religious beliefs or political ideologies. It would probably have been better for him/her to keep quiet or make sure whatever he/she says does not compromise his/her human rights activism. It does not mean he/she has to be a people pleaser. No, we should be ready to condemn whatever is wrong, and that should never mean we don't care.

As earlier stated, my unique message is that love, peace, and respect for diversity are the most important virtues we should all embrace if we want to make our world a great place to live in. It might seem easy to stick to this message and stick to it in all my communications and behaviors, but it's not. I'm human. I have emotions and the right to express those emotions. I reflect on issues and realities and exercise my freedom to express my thoughts. How do I justify my anger without sending a message of hate to those I'm angry at? How do I express my emotions of sadness, without provoking remorse feelings in those who saddened me, but simply because I'm human? I believe the most important is to formulate your personal message and make sure you use it to evaluate whatever you do, say, or write. It does not mean your behaviors or words shall never be scrutinized or judged. It should not only be what people conclude, but what you said or did. It's not about one word or one action, but all put together should convey your full message, instead of contradicting each other.

There are two elements of an excellent unique personal message, clarity and consistency. Your unique personal message should be evident through your written and spoken words, behaviors, etiquette, and actions. Unfortunately, people sometimes label us with what we do not want to be associated with, and the only way we should react to this is by making sure they receive the message we want to communicate.

There is a word of caution here. I do not mean that you should communicate what people want you to communicate. I suggest you should communicate what you want to communicate, as long as it's worth communicating. It may not be what the world wants to hear but what it should be aware of.

Having a unique personal message is for everyone. Whatever the profession you are in, there is that message you convey when people interact with you. When you do not decide this, you may either communicate different conflicting messages, or get mistaken for who you may not be, and not who you really are and want to be known as.

We know people who may have earned some labels not because they chose so, but because their words, behaviors, and actions communicate that message. A hater is not necessarily the person who says, "I hate you." It might be any person who expresses negative wishes for another person, verbally abuses him/her, or physically assaults him/her. Some people are known to be combative when others are known for being peaceful. Some are known to be extremists, others as impartial. Believe me, when I tell you that some of those labeled combative probably wish to be labeled conciliatory, and those labeled extremists wished the world knew they were impartial. The only thing they don't know is how those who judge their behaviors and actions came up with these labels, and what they should do to make sure their words and behaviors convey the message of peace, or impartiality, if that's indeed what they mean.

When defining your unique personal message, it's vital to grasp the secret of starting with an end in mind. What is your life purpose? What contribution do you want to make to the betterment of the world? How do you want to do it? Once you understand this, you should make sure that your words, behaviors, etiquette, and actions communicate that message.

In my work as a Human Resources Professional, I receive a lot of colleagues coming to complain about the fact that their work efforts are not recognized. I am a strong advocate for performance recognition and reward.

However, in some cases, I need to explain to employees that it's not only about how much you deliver but also how you deliver. I worked in an organization that respected diversity and ensured that its Human Resources policies do not have any clause that jeopardizes diversity and inclusion. We did not have a dress code. However, some staff members found themselves being informally judged based on how they dressed. Most of them would come to ask what dress code was accepted. My simple response was that we might not have a dress code but a dress culture. While a dress code may be specified, a dress culture is not always written. As new or junior staff members, they just needed to observe the people they want to be identified with, and learn from them. Imagine you have to attend a summit of presidents and government ministers of different countries. Would you not guess how you should dress to fit in? Shall you not think about how to behave in those circles? The same applies to other jobs, professions, or professional communities. You might need to speak, behave, and act in a way associated with what you do, unless your message is about changing possibilities, proving the importance of diversity, or protesting against conservatism. The point I am making is that it's not only your words and behaviors that should communicate your message, but also your appearance and everything you do. It does not have to be the clichés, like dreadlocks, tattoos, suits and ties, etc., unless you like them, but whatever you think uniquely conveys your message.

Personal brand and branding

We assume that you have already formulated your unique personal message. The next step is to understand that you are the brand that shall communicate this message. What do you want people to feel when they hear your name? Companies use their names, logos, mottos, and slogans as branding strategies to communicate their unique selling proposition. As an individual, what tools do you use to communicate your unique personal message?

Before we discuss branding, let's understand the meaning of a brand. A brand is the image associate with your name. It is who people think you are. It's influenced by the extent to which you meet their expectations of you, how memorable their experiences with you are, and the quality of their relationships with you. You may use different tools to influence this brand, but the tools should not be mistaken for being the brand. Sometimes the tools convey the right unique personal message and influence your brand the way you want. Sometimes the tools communicate a message that does not match the brand you want to create. Sometimes, you define well your unique personal message, but your brand conveys another message.

So after deciding your unique personal message, you will work to make sure that your brand conveys this message. To do this, you will use different tools and methods, and what you will be doing is called "branding," which is simply the process of influencing your brand. It encompasses all those words, actions, tools, methods, and channels you use to influence the people's expectations of you and their memories of experiences with you. It's about affecting the image they associate with you.

You should note the difference between personal branding and self-promotion. Many people mistake personal branding for self-promotion. All they do is use online tools such as social media or offline tools such as TV, radios, and newspapers for self-promotion, not necessarily branding. Those who understand the difference, between the two, focus more on their interactions with people and make sure they leave an image that matches the message they want to communicate. These may use the same online and offline tools, not to talk about themselves, but to effectively interact with their audience and make those interactions as memorable as possible. The objective should not be about how many people know you, but the image people associate with their interactions with you.

Many personal coaches may judge your branding efforts by only looking at how many followers you have in the different social media, how many applaud and talk about what you do, or how many people buy your services. All these are useful metrics, but they do not tell the whole story. Let me tell you something; I'm not talking about having many followers on social media or views on your online videos. I am talking about how significant and memorable your interactions with other people, few or many, are. Does the image they associate with those interactions match the message you want to convey? It's not about your popularity, but the effectiveness of what you do. There are so many people out there who have a lot of fans and followers, but you may feel like you never want to communicate the same messages they convey or behave the same way they do, however popular it might be. Your message may not be the most prevalent, but the most important to you. If you are convinced that your message is essential, get it across. Let it reach those that it's intended for. They may be only two or ten people, a million, a billion, or the entire humanity. What shall determine your brand's success is whether those who received your message understood it the way you intended. There are many tools you can use for branding. However, always remember that the most important is social interaction with people, face-to-face, or online.

The following are three methods you can use to influence your brand:

- Physical interactions: When interacting with people, bear in mind that first impressions matter. Use every opportunity to convey your unique personal message. Do not only use words. Make sure your voice, gestures, and appearance, carry the same message. Remember that it's essential to be authentic and genuine. Project a professional presence. Show empathy. People will only want to relate to you because they know you care. Use your first and last name. Make good eye contact, give a firm handshake, and make a clear and concise introduction. That's the most effective tool for your personal branding efforts. People relate to people and not with computers or papers. Make an effort to interact with different people, and more specifically, with your target audience.
- Offline written communications: There are sever-

al tools in this category that you can use to convey your unique personal message. These include, but are not limited to; business cards, postcards, posters, a biography, a resume, etc. When using this method, make sure you are as brief and as concise as possible. Understand the power of color and use it to your advantage. If you are distributing these, do it to create relationships and not to advertise yourself. Remember, people will want to continue interacting with you, not because they know you and you make sure they never forget you, but because they like what they experience when they interact with you.

- Online communication: There are so many tools you may use to communicate your unique personal message online. The most effective channel today is social media. The success of using social media has been cheapened to having many followers. If you only would like to get followers or fans, you can communicate anything, as long as it attracts many people. I don't think that's what you want. You communicate to connect. You want to reach out to those who have an interest in your message. You are not targeting everybody. You are genuinely sharing your values, interests, and contributions to make our world a better place. Yes, you want to reach out to as many people as possible, not to be famous, but for your message to reach most of those intended. Apart from social media, you can use a personal website, a blog, emails, online videos, etc. The same principles apply; so be as brief and concise as possible. Use colors, fonts, and layouts to your advantage. Portray professionalism in all your communications. Don't be fake; be genuine.

People and networking

We are all part of different networks of people. These may be our families, circles of friends, social, political, or religious communities, professional colleagues, suppliers, potential suppliers, clients, potential clients, sponsors, supporters, etc. We should keep in mind that interacting effectively with people in our networks always offers opportunities. People do business with those they know, like, and trust. The sooner you realize this, the more effective you shall be in making sure your interactions with other people contribute to fulfilling your life purpose.

I have interacted with many people in my work as a Human Resources Professional, and in my creative journey as a writer. Some people complain that nobody notices their talents or is ready to support them. That's somehow half the truth. Maybe nobody notices, but this does not mean that none wants to notice if he/she was given a chance to. The only problem here is that you may be creative and have a lot you can share with society, but you never let people get to know you, trust you, listen to your unique personal message and choose to be part of it.

When I say this, some people think that I mean the publicized networking approach of going to different places, introducing yourself, and distributing business cards. That's good, but it's not enough. Do not get frustrated when you learn that a lot of people shall not even remember where they shall have thrown your business cards. At workplaces, many people think about networking as stepping out to different offices sometimes to talk nonsense. No. That's not networking.

So then what's networking, and how does it link to your success as a creative person? Networking is about thinking beyond yourself as an individual and seeing yourself as part of a bigger group of those who share your interests, passions, and values. It's about making sure you take advantage of what you have in common with these people and help each other be the best you can become. It's about being where you are supposed to be, with whom you are supposed to be, and when you are supposed to be there. It's about sharing and giving to those that have an interest in what you are offering. Is your aim to be an actor? Go to Hollywood! What do I mean by Hollywood? I mean to go where you will find actors, movie producers, and directors. You will never be a successful actor in the kitchen of your house. Do you want to be a politician? Join a political party. Do you want to write a book? Start by reading books and sharing experiences with both book readers and authors. Do you want to be a designer? Network with other designers; let them learn from your ideas and learn something from them as well.

We are very fortunate that nowadays, there are so many opportunities to grab for us to network with the people that may contribute to our success in one way or another. They are not only those who sponsor us with money, nor those who pull us up and introduce us to our profession's higher levels. They include people who encourage us with their words of wisdom, their pieces of advice, and their great ideas on how things are done or should be done. They include people who listen to us when we feel like talking and speak when we feel like listening. Some of the tools we may use to connect with these people include online tools such as websites, blogs, and social media. They also include offline social interactions around a sports activity, different clubs of those who share our interests, e.g., cooking clubs, book clubs, prayer groups, etc. The only problem is that networking has been so publicized with another connotation to the extent of making it sound like a risky business.

When you interact with people in your networks, please remember that every person you meet has a message he/she wants to get across, and personal goals he/she wants to achieve. Your aim should not be to tell other people whatever you want to say to them, because they are too preoccupied with their situations and may not empathetically listen to you. Your aim should be to connect with them. It's by showing them you care and empathetically listening to them that they will want to stay connected with you. Listen and learn from their experiences; understand their needs, go with the flow until you reach a point when you can offer solutions to their problems.

Another thing we have already talked about is that you have to be genuine and not fake. No one will want to connect with you if you keep many rooms in your life shuttered. People shall only connect with you because you have let them discover who you are and realize what you can offer.

Below are things you may do to expand your networks and stay connected:

- Volunteer to share your expertise and ideas: It maybe with your friends, at your workplace, in the cooking club, sports team; association; and any other social community.
- Learn, unlearn, and relearn: Be the first to acquire knowledge and skills in your expertise area. Learn from other people's experiences.
- Be visible: It's all about your visibility. The world is too busy to search for you if you are not visible. Show yourself offline and online. If you are an artist, expect to be in the gatherings of artists. If you chose to be a computer scientist, be in their midst. Stay in touch with people. Communicate consistently.
- Do not only connect with people; build relationships: Don't focus on yourself. Learn and understand their needs and interests. Be a good listener and give heartedly.

Resources and finances

I am from one of the poorest countries on the globe and with a very young population. Most of these young adults have only one excuse for not making it. Their justification for not turning their creative potential into success is a lack of finances. Most of them are right. These young people are in an economy where no banks accept to finance startups with no collateral. The few banks that finance startups request for collateral. The economy has no angel investors, no sponsors, and no easy ways of collecting capital money. It is indeed a big challenge for them. However, I believe the solution lies again within these young creative people.

Although I understand the situation of those who find themselves with no money to venture into any business, I also wonder who told them that they needed money to make money. I do not believe that it should always be the case. I have seen people who made money with no money. I, myself, was once one of those. After the death of my father and my two elder brothers, my mother, my sisters, and I joined a traditional dance troupe. We loved it! It was fun! We needed it as therapy after our father's death, and the aim was not to make money. A few months later, we were paying school fees with the money we earned from dancing. Another experience is when I was given a job by a Kigali lady, to distribute for sale clothes she imported from abroad. She would set the minimum price, and my pay was the difference from my bargained sale price and the minimum I would bring to her. I was a teenager and gratified by the fact that I could buy clothes from the money I had earned. My younger brother, who is a visual artist, when he started, he used special tools; dust and eye pencils. When he started earning from his paintings, he widened his toolbox to include those I do not want to name because I don't know well how they are called. I hear words such as oil, acrylic, and pastels. Once in a while, depending on where his creativity takes him and his clients' needs, he uses other traditional techniques. He did not wait for the day he would get money to buy some of the modern tools he uses today. He decided to use the nature-given tools to start his creation. All you probably need to do is look at your surroundings; there could be opportunities you may grab.

Let's think of a lady who has only $5. She is called Chantal. She decides to buy a crochet hook and yarn and make tablecloths. Some people notice what she does and contracts her to make tablecloths for them. In the old days, people used to put coverings on their living room tables. With the money she makes from her small business, Chantal takes care of the three younger siblings she is raising after their parents' death. One day, she realizes that the money from crocheting is not enough. She decides to invest in a tailoring machine and approach her friends who mastered tailoring. Chantal has one unique asset; her creativity. She can draw, and her designs are excellent. She creates a website and social media pages on which she showcases her designs. At her church, she makes sure other believers know about her new venture as a tailor. She communicates the same to the clients of her crocheted tablecloths. Many people come to Chantal to seek advice on the designs that match their body shapes. Satisfied clients refer others to her. Her income is increasing, and she has many other exciting projects and plans. She does not want to be contented by just being a tailor for her community. She wants to be a renowned specialist in haute couture.

Some young people are probably more fortunate than Strong Karakire and Chantal, but they don't realize it. Some of them have graduated with degrees in different domains. Some are computer scientists; others are architects; others graduated from business administration, etc. I commend those who did not wait for somebody to read their resumes and offer them jobs. I salute those who have ventured into producing innovative products, despite the challenges in their environment. Some of them have ventured into the music industry; others have ventured into art; others are using their information technology skills to create ways of connecting people; others are in the fashion industry. I commend these young people. However, I note that we still have many who think that there is nothing they can do since they have no money. A lot of young people are ambitious, and this is good. But the ambition should push them to move instead of waiting for the day they would be able to jump. They should think big, but start small!

Below are a few tips that can help the young people who would like to start the quest to turn their creative potential into success, despite the fact that they have no finances:

- Think about what you are good at. In step #2, we have looked at your mental abilities. In step #3, we have looked at the personality traits that may be pushing you or pulling you back. In step #4, we have discussed your interests, personal drive, and needs as your possible motivators. Now you know what you are good at and what interests you; what Sir Ken Robinson, a guru in creativity, calls 'The element'. Start from your element.
- Start by offering your talents to others. Do not rush to set a price. Start by proving what you can do, and when people show interest, communicate the price.
- Acquire more knowledge and skills. Learn from others. There are so many people out there who

will be happy to share their experiences with you. Do not only look for the well-established people. Start from your friends who master one or two things you do not. Who knows? Maybe playing the piano in your friend's living room may be the starting point for your music career.
- Be entrepreneurial. It's disappointing to meet a young person with no projects whatsoever. It's all about exchanges. You will only advance yourself the day you shall grasp you have to give to receive. Think about the needs of people in your market, then create products to satisfy those needs.
- Spend less; save more. Have you started earning a little money? That's is the time you should start saving. I bet you if you do not save now, you will not save when you are earning hundreds of thousands of dollars. Set a target and save to reach that target.
- Invest in your small business; I have seen people starting a small shop in their neighborhood when the aim is to venture into real estate. I have seen those beginning with a barbershop and ending up with a supermarket.
- Re-invest your earnings. To grow your business, you will need to learn the concept of saving money to invest.
- It's not only those who are unfortunate not to have money that should strategize on their resources and finances. It is useful for all of us who want to turn our creative potential into success.
- A lot of business ventures do not last for more than two years. Do you know why? That's because

many people put all their money into the initial investment, thinking that they will be making a profit after one month. No. It's is nearly impossible. You will need to write your business plan and do some financial forecasts. If you would like to quit your current job and start your own business, make sure you have saved all you need to start, plus an amount that is equivalent to 24 months of expenses. That shall give you peace of mind that you will not only rely on making profits to sustain your household.
- Use any money you make to meet your overheads, then save or re-invest any surplus. You should let the power of compound interest work for you. A lot of us let this power only work for the banks. It should not be the case.
- Diversify with caution: Don't put all your eggs in one basket, but choose where to invest with caution. Start with one area that you are more interested in. Do not start any other venture before you break even in the previous one.
- If you are currently employed, do not quit your full-time job before you have a plan that shall work.
- Think big, start small: The fact that you have money or can afford something does not mean that you should start big. There are so many factors that should influence your decision. Are you an expert in that area? Have you done it before? Have you done some market research and intelligence? How significant is the risk? How are you prepared to manage the risks, if any?

Draw your strategies

As earlier stated, a strategy is a pattern of decisions and actions directed towards achieving your goals. There are so many decisions you will need to make. There are so many actions you will take in order to achieve your goals. The most important ones we have discussed are:

- Formulating your unique personal message;
- Creating, communicating, and influencing your brand;
- Interacting with people and building networks;
- Managing resources and finances.

At this juncture, I believe that you are now clear about your creative potential, the kind of success you want to achieve, and the strategies you will adopt to achieve success. I believe you are now ready to take the 7th step and embark on your creative production!

STEP 7

Embark on Creative Production

In step 6, we looked at how you should strategize to achieve your goals. We discussed the importance of determining your unique personal message, the brand you want to create, and the methods you may apply to influence your brand. We also looked at how you can leverage the synergy among people as one of the strategies to achieve your goals. Last but not least, we discussed how we should manage our resources and finances to keep moving towards achieving our goals.

In step 7, you are still in the creative workshop and are now ready to kick off the production. We will discuss how you generate creative ideas, visualize and illustrate your creative plans, produce and package your creative products, and finally release and distribute them.

After this step, you will have understood the process a creative person goes through to produce novel products. Let's start with inspiration and idea generation.

Inspiration and idea generation
The first stage of any creative production is about inspiration and idea generation.

What do we mean by inspiration? There are divergent theories on inspiration. Some people believe inspiration is a divine and mystical phenomenon. Others believe it is a result of a random unison of thoughts in a person's mind. Our take should be that inspiration is unconscious thought about something that happened or could happen. It is unplanned and unexpected. A creative person may be walking in an open market, and, out of the blue, he/she experiences the burst of thought related to how his surroundings are or should be. He may also have inspiration for something that has nothing to do with that market. Inspiration is not a process but a random occurrence.

On the other hand, idea generation is a process that may either result from inspiration or be intended, planned, and independent of any random, divine, or mystical thought. Some people may be inspired to do something, but before they decide to sit down and think about what they should do and how they should do it, no change shall happen. Idea generation should be intentional for any creative person who wants to achieve success in his/her creative endeavors.

Let's use an example to understand it. You may be looking up in the sky and observing the moon, and suddenly you think of making an object with the shape of a moon. That's an inspiration. You may decide to ignore that thought and go on with your life. You may continue to think about that shape and wonder if any object can be of that shape. Then, you decide to take time to reflect more on it. When you get into your house, you sit down, and take a pen and paper, and start writing down what can have the shape of the moon you saw. That's the idea generation.

A scenario of when idea generation may be independent of random inspiration would be: You're an architect, and one day you meet Mr. Francis. He tells you that he would like you to suggest designs for the new house he wants to build. He requests you to propose some creative house designs he might consider. You decide to sit in your office and generate ideas. You shall think about designs that meet Mr. Francis' needs and preferences. You shall probably take time to study the plot on which he wants to build his house and the surrounding landscape. You shall probably collect ideas from friends or browse the internet for ideas. What you want to achieve is coming up with a long list of ideas you can play with, compare, combine, change, customize, adapt, or reject. You have not yet decided on one design to propose to Mr. Francis. You're still generating and evaluating ideas.

There are many idea generation techniques creative people use. For example:

- Mind mapping: Writing down all ideas and connecting with a line each idea to another or other ideas related to it.
- Brainstorming: If you have a team, you may ask them to say or write down their ideas. It would help to collect as many ideas as possible.
- The 5W+H Method: Asking yourself the fundamental questions about whatever you would like to do: Who, what, where, when, why, and how?
- Attribute listing: Breaking the idea into parts and

analyzing each component's features and functions to identify improvement areas.
- Forced relationships: Joining totally different ideas to come up with a fresh idea.
- Reverse thinking: Reversing the idea and ask yourself what could happen if things were done in the opposite way, or what could happen if you aimed for the opposite result.
- Questioning assumptions: Questioning the deeply-held beliefs about how things should be, and wondering what could happen if you had gone against those beliefs.

The exercise to generate and evaluate your ideas shall lead you to identify the best from a long list of ideas.

A lot of people get inspiration and never engage in the deliberate idea generation process. These people are those who say, "Ah, I also thought about it." Other people are those who are convergent thinkers. One idea clicks in their mind, and there they go; they start the production. Idea generation is a crucial stage of any creative production.

In whatever you do, you should learn to generate as many ideas as possible and evaluate them using as many methods as possible. It's not enough to have an inspiration. Sit and write down your thoughts. Come up with different scenarios and evaluate them objectively. The most creative people understand the secret of generating many ideas, then make comparisons and combinations, add and subtract, and enjoy the mental process of playing with ideas.

Another group of people is of those who wait to get inspiration to do something creative. Yes, inspiration may lead to idea generation, but in itself, it may be insufficient. Whereas on the other hand, idea generation may be independent of inspiration. To generate creative ideas, one has to engage in a process to reflect on the different ways to solve problems and devise the necessary courses of action.

In the first part of this book, we have looked at the different mental abilities associated with creative potential. However, the fact that a person has these cognitive abilities does not guarantee that he/she shall engage in a successful creative production. We have also discussed the personality traits that lead the person to move from just having the creative potential to embarking into a creative process. These include the person's curiosity to venture into new creative production processes and enjoy the flow of ideas without worrying about being efficient. All of these won't serve your creativity if you do not invest time and effort in generating creative ideas.

Idea generation is the first step in the creative production process and the most important. Other people can produce too, but the difference between those who simply produce and those who do it creatively is the novelty, quality, and usefulness of their ideas. Creative people enjoy this process of generating ideas. Creative people engage in divergent thinking and enjoy the music of how ideas flow in their minds. Creative people relish the mental process of evaluating ideas, identifying linkages, compare, and combine. Creative people generate and evaluate ideas.

Visualization and illustration

At this stage of the creative production process, the creative person shall visualize his/her idea's possible outcome. It is about mentally visualizing the final product. We have combined this with the process of illustration. After mentally visualizing the possible outcome, the creative person shall draw a sketch or a graphical representation of his/her products. In the business world, this is the stage of writing a business plan or a project proposal. In the movie industry, this is the stage when the person shall write a script or a screenplay.

Visualization and illustration is equally a critical stage. It is about bridging from idea generation to the actual production of creative objects.

A lot of people come up with great ideas but never pay attention to the process of mapping out their creative production. Failure to visualize your final product before you embark on the production may lead to non-success in your creative endeavors, even if you had generated some great ideas.

Imagine a lady who came up with different ideas for a movie. She has generated and evaluated many ideas and picked the best. She has written the script herself, and apparently, it has all the details. She decides she needs no other producer; she shall do it herself. She finds two or three people to be part of the crew. She does not tell them precisely what they will do. The most important thing is to have a camera and some people to do the casting, she thinks. They start shooting the movie, but later on, she realizes that there are two characters that she did not find actors for. She also notices that she does not like the way the sets are built. She wants to re-do the shooting. Where did she go wrong? Was there anything wrong with her movie idea? What would you advise her to do?

The lady probably had a great movie idea. However, she missed the step of mapping out the production process before the shooting. In the process of visualizing the movie's shooting, she could have come up with different ideas on how to build and decorate the sets. She could have figured out how many people she needed for both the crew and the cast. She could have determined who was going to take which casting role. The lady had probably a fantastic idea, but failed to map it out and plan her production.

This stage is generally about planning how to turn your creative idea into a creative product. It's about visualizing and mapping out your creative production process. When people ask me how long it takes me to write a book, I give them different responses. It takes several months from thinking about writing a book on a specific topic and finally deciding on the story idea. I often have different story ideas to choose from, and since I cannot write all of them simultaneously, I pick one. However, having a story to tell is not enough. Before sitting down to write, I outline the central plots, decide on the setting, and create believable characters, with different personalities, experiences, values, and lifestyles.

Sometimes we are forced to follow different sketches, plans, and steps that may dilute our creativity, and many creative people find this like being asked to think within a particular box. It would be best to keep in mind that laziness is not one of the characteristics of creative people. I encourage you always to sit down, map out your ideas, give them a form, and visualize the final product before you embark on any creative production.

Production and packaging

You have generated and evaluated your ideas. You have visualized the creative objects that shall come out of your creative production process. Now you are going to start the actual production. You are going to start the actual cooking. A cook comes up with a meal idea, decides the ingredients, the quantities, and the sequence. Then, he/she embarks on cooking. The same applies to any creative production. After mapping out his/her ideas and visualizing the possible products, the creative person kicks off the production. A friend of mine is a tailor and a fashion designer. He has so many great ideas. I like to tell him that he has it in his blood. He can simply look at you and advise the fashion design that can go with your body shape and skin tone. He has excellent creative ideas, and that's good. On top of having great ideas, I see him engaging in the production process. He will enter his workshop, sometimes close the door, and start tailoring. In the end, what gets out of that workshop is incredible. We can also take the example of web developers. The guys sit in front of their computers and literally develop the websites. They invest time, effort, and other resources in their creative production. If you need more examples to understand what I mean, you can talk to musicians. They will tell you how long it takes to write a song and fit the words into the melody. How tiresome it is to record the audio. When the music is ready, they also add many hours of planning and shooting the song video.

As a writer, I can have the best story idea, outline it,

decide on the setting and the characters, but if I don't sit down and write, no story shall be written, and nobody shall ever read my stories.

I would like you to remember that ideas cannot be touched, heard, seen, smelled, or tasted. For ideas to be touched, they have to be translated into tangible objects. For ideas to be heard, they have to be translated into audible objects. For ideas to be seen, they have to be translated into seeable objects. For ideas to be smelled, they have to be translated into scented objects. For ideas to be savored, they have to be translated into flavorsome objects.

Any creative person should keep in mind the following:

- It's cooking, and you are the cook: The first aim of the cook is to get a quality meal for his/her guest. He/she will make sure he/she does not miss any detail that would change the taste, color, or the aroma of his/her meal.
- Time is the essential resource: Find that quality time to work on your project. Please do not give it the residual time. Don't rush; it may hinder quality. Don't prolong the time; you need to deliver when it's still relevant.
- Quality is key: Yes, you have those great ideas but remember that once you translate them into products, the market shall evaluate them. Please, make sure you give the best you can.
- It's an investment, so treat it as such: I know you have already invested time and effort, but if there is any dollar, you have to get out of your pocket. Do not hesitate. You are giving to yourself and the world.

- Quantity reaches out: Quality gets you the best clients; quantity gets you many clients. Do not forget that. Have you released a song, work on the second and the third. Have you written a book, write another one.

Production is always followed by packaging. I had a team member, Nadia, who complained that I was demanding, not only on the content of her reports but on the form and style. In her words, I put more emphasis on the packaging. She always argued that what matters is the content and not the font, colors, formats, etc. of her reports. I reminded her that even for food, what matters is not only the taste and the nutritional value but how it's served on the plate and the table. It took me a lot of effort and energy to explain to Nadia that it mattered how she packaged her work.

As a creative person, you should invest in packaging your creative work. I often tell people that eyes are closest to the brain than any other organ. Maybe it's not true. But I think that if you want to influence the brain, you should start by what your eyes see. Marketers know this well. They understand the importance of packaging. Look at the cars we drive. Most of them are similar if we only consider the inside and the technologies applied in vehicles' construction. But the packaging is different, and a lot of laypeople do not check other features of cars but the packaging.

Whenever I decide to buy a car, I always know the brand and model I want because I saw it and liked it. Luckily, my husband understands some of the other car specifications we should check. I never allow him to buy a car that looks ugly, even if he tells me that I will be taking it for a safari. Look at phones and computers. Some companies have understood the secret. They work at both the inside and the outside. Imagine a good musician with a pleasant voice, who would stand, her back facing a white wall in her kitchen, to sing and record a song video. She shall probably make different music recordings and sell them for money. However, she should be prepared for the fact that buyers may only judge the packaging and pay her the maximum they can pay for home-made videos with a simple white background.

Many people end their contribution from just having great ideas and letting other people implement their ideas. However, when you do that, if you are lucky enough, you only share 10% of the success. The person who will pick up your creative idea and engage in a process to add value on it shall receive more credit. I do not mean that you should never share your thoughts with others. You should always share your creative ideas and receive creative ideas from others. I am talking to you and assuming that you already understand that you are creative and you would like to turn this creative potential into success. The value you add to your creative ideas by turning them into creative products is incredible, and I encourage you not to ignore it, if it leads to the achievement of your goals and the accomplishment of your life purpose.

Release and distribution

You have already gone through the first stage of inspiration and idea generation in the creative production process. You have also gone through the second stage of visualization and illustration, and finally, you have picked up your tools and started the actual production process. Very good! Assume you now have your well-packaged creative products, and you would like to sell to your target population.

Are you a comedian and want to contribute by giving people an opportunity to laugh as a way of coping with the challenges of this world? Are you a pharmacologist, and you would like to make sure people have access to effective treatment? Are you a computer scientist and would like to give people the tools to make their lives easier? Are you a musician and you want to use your music to entertain people and soothe their minds? Do you want to use your comedy, medical inventions, IT applications, music, and art to communicate an important message to the world? Are you a writer, and you would like to use your writing to convey a critical message? Whatever profession you are in, and whatever creative process you may engage in, the end result shall not be producing creative products, but to make sure your products reach those they are intended for and serve the purpose they are created for. To make an impact, you need to make sure whoever needs your creative products can easily access them. The more people you reach, the better. What you probably need to think about is how, when, and where to distribute your products to the targeted population.

Release and distribution is the challenge of many people, including writers like me. There are decisions you will have to make. These are not only the distribution channels but also other choices related to pricing and marketing. Below are the elements you should think about when devising your release and distribution strategy:

- Pricing: Are you releasing your creative objects for a price? If yes, what do you aim at achieving with this price? Do you only want to cover your costs of production? Do you want to make a profit? What is the reasonable profit margin you aim at? What's the affordable price that your target market shall be able to pay? How much are other people/companies delivering similar products charging?
- Marketing campaigns: I believe by now, you have started building your brand and have taken different steps into personal branding. How about your products? Are they going to have individual brands, or will you be trading them under your brand? What channels shall you use for marketing your products? Have you thought about online marketing? Have you thought about offline marketing? How are you going to advertise your products?
- Distribution channels: Last but not least, what distribution channels are you going to use? Shall you sell in physical retail shops? Shall you sell through online channels? Shall you deliver on-demand? How are you going to reach clients that are in different geographical areas? How are you going to get to clients with varying preferences in terms of how they want the products to be delivered to them?

As a writer, when it comes to the release and distribution of my books, stories, poems, I always have many options to consider and choose from. Some writers decide to search for a literary agency that shall link them up with a traditional publisher, before considering self-publishing. Some others prefer to hire the services of a self-publishing company or a hybrid publisher, without going through a literary agent. Some others go for the DIY. Whatever option the writers go for, there are still decisions they make and actions they take to make sure their books, or any other written products, reach as many people as possible. What I have come to understand, readers do not only buy our books; they respond to our call for a conversation, and the writer has to be ready to keep the conversation on. The same applies to other creative people. Whenever we like a song, we often want to know more about the singer. Whenever we like painting, we want to know what was on the artist's mind when he/she painted it. As a creator, you have to master the art of interacting with your target audience.

I have seen creative people from the part of the world I come from complaining that they did something and nobody was willing to pay for what they did. Many of these are those who produced great creative products but failed to invest time and effort in the marketing and distribution of their products. For example, in Rwanda, I have interacted with musicians who claimed that the Media never promoted their music. My question to them, which has never adequately been answered, is: Why do I see other commercials on TV channels? Has the Media refused to receive your money to advertise their music? Do you have a marketing plan? How much have you budgeted for the marketing and promotion of your products? However, this has started to change. The music industry in my country is booming more than other creative industries. They are doing wonders. I wished it was the same for creative writers in my country. We are still struggling. Rwanda musicians have now expanded their distribution channels to include well-performing music streaming and media services providers and other online music sellers.

You do not have to spend a fortune on marketing and distributing your products. Depending on which marketing campaign or distribution channel you choose, you should spend enough time, effort, and more money on ensuring that your target audience is not only aware of the existence of your products, but is also motivated to buy. In this interdependent world, we all have only one question in mind: "What is in it for me?" The Media shall never refuse to advertise your creative work as long as they see "what is in it for them." If your products meet the target population's needs, those who shall use or consume them shall refer them to others. People shall buy from you not to do you a favor, but because they see "what is in it for them."

However, as much as you need to invest time and effort in your products' marketing and distribution, you should keep in mind that the most effective marketing tool is 'your product.' The more quality products you release, the more people they will reach. I'm a witness to this. When I published a second book, I was surprised to see that my first book's sales also increased. It was as if the second book sold the first book as well. As you market, promote and distribute your products, remember to produce more. Another advice I would like to give you is that you should be realistic and understand that you cannot start today and reach success tomorrow. Yes, miracles do happen, but they would not be called miracles if they were for everyone. Do not be discouraged if success does not happen overnight. Remember, you have a purpose to accomplish and an important message to communicate. Please, do not dilute it for the sake of popularity, fame, or money.

End of Part II

From creative potential to a creativity workshop. Congratulations! You are making significant steps towards turning your creative potential into success.

In the first part of this book, we reviewed the first four steps.

Step #1 was about understanding your situation. It was about thinking about the way you view the world, its people, and yourself. You have understood how the conclusions you may have drawn about the world, its people, and yourself affect your creative potential and your ability to turn it into success.

Step #2 took you through assessing your actual creative potential by discovering your mental abilities and how these link to your creative potential.

Step #3 was about understanding your personality traits, how these contribute to your creative potential, and the role they play in your quest to turning your creative potential into success.

Step #4 took you through the motivation factors

that may be pushing you towards turning your creative potential into success.

The second part of this book was about entering a creativity workshop in order to translate your creative potential into creative ideas and products.

Step #5 helped you formulate your life purpose statement and set the goals you want to achieve in your creative journey.

Step #6 took you through the process of drawing strategies for the achievement of your goals and the accomplishment of your life purpose.

Step #7 took you through the actual generation of creative ideas and the production of creative products.

At this juncture, you do not only have creative potential; you have been able to put it at work to produce creative products. You have done this after discovering your creative potential, deciding the purpose to accomplish with this creative potential, and engaging in a process to produce creative ideas and products. There is no way we could be talking of success if you had not made these steps.

Part #3 of this book shall take you through the process of maintaining that point of success and making sure that the only way to move from there is by moving forward. We shall take you through this guide's last three steps, which are about success and sustainability.

PART III

SUCCESS & SUSTAINABILITY

STEP 8

Fight with Creativity Killers

I have never met any single person whose decision to pursue success from nothing else, but his/her creative potential, was approved by all the people in his/her surroundings. Most of the time, it's just that one voice that tells you, "go for it, girl!" or "go for it, boy." Many people shall say to you that you do not have what it takes to do it. Others shall remind you of the mistakes you made in the past and caution you about ending up making the same mistakes. Others shall want you to do it their way and not your way. Others simply think it's risky and would like to advise you to go the more comfortable way. However, the most influential person who discourages you is that little voice inside you that pulls information from the pessimistic you and tries to shut up the voice that gets erudition from the optimistic you.

Some authors state that we all have "fear of the unknown." Yes, we do, but that fear did not prevent us from coming to a world we had never seen before. It did not stop people from deciding to walk on the moon. It did not stop us from coming up with different inventions such as hydroelectricity. It did not stop us from making airplanes that sometimes kill many. Who could have ever imagined that the Wright brothers' kite in 1899 would lead to the plane we know today?

There are so many realities that oppressed your creativity or even attempted to kill it since you were a child. Remember that voice that always told you no. Remember when you felt as if you were not allowed to be who you are and do what pleases you. Was it as if the school's purpose was to make you fit in the thinking box designed for you? You were taught that you could either be right or wrong. You were taught that you should sit when others are seated, stand up when they do, be in blue when they are in blue. The teacher knew everything, and you were supposed to rely on his knowledge. When you moved to college, you thought you were going to embrace the universe and think freely. Instead of encouraging you to expand your thinking horizons, university professors added more theories you always have to refer to, even though some of those theories may have been written by those who decided to use their thinking capabilities properly. They told you that all you should do was compare and contrast those theories, instead of reinventing the wheel, as if innovation was not encouraged.

Today, it seems as if you no longer need other people to criticize you. You have learned how to do that yourself. Did I say that you should never evaluate your ideas or work? No. I said it should not stop there. The worst response you can ever get from somebody is, "You cannot do it," or "That's impossible." It's worse when you get these responses from your own voice. What you should rather say to yourself is, "It seems difficult, so to make it, I will need to be a little bit more creative." Instead of being told that you have not what it takes to do it, you should be told what you might do to make it happen.

Let's look at the different creativity killers.

The Guru

The word 'guru' means a 'teacher' or an 'imparter of knowledge.' We interact with these people on different occasions. Some are real gurus, and others simply believe they are. One thing these people have in common is that they have knowledge and expertise in particular domains. They may have acquired this knowledge and expertise through education or experience. They have drawn conclusions based on their knowledge and experience, and may not be flexible enough to change them. It's vital to mingle with these people and learn from them. They have a lot to teach you. They are invaluable sources of knowledge.

Then how do they become creativity killers? We have already defined creativity as the ability to come up with new and creative ideas and products. These must be things that people did not experience before or some transformations of what people already know. A creative person does not stop on the statement of "This is how we always did it." A creative person understands how we always did it and thinks about how we can do it better or differently. A creative person keeps a fresh mind, even though experiences may influence some of his/her ideas. A creative person knows that yesterday's realities are different from today's realities and that today's realities might be different from those of tomorrow.

One of the many skills my mother taught me is

dancing our traditional music. I loved the way she danced. However, when I grew up, I noticed that not everybody danced like my mother. Even in my country that is believed to have a homogenous culture, people from different parts of the country danced differently. Many young people found themselves in the cities with influence from different parts of the country, if not parts of the world. Today, I have seen people mixing different sorts of dances in one song, and many people like it. Some dances were considered loud and requiring so much energy, and those who preferred soft music did not like them. Some other dances were judged melodious, and these are the ones my mother considered to be the authentic Rwandan music. Today, the young generations have mixed many features of Rwandan traditional music to meet the different needs of their audiences. My mother was believed to be a master in traditional dancing, and yes, indeed, she was. What she did not understand is that things can be done differently.

For any activity we engage in, there are always gurus in that profession, and sometimes these tell us that we cannot do what we want to do if we do not get the gurus' approval. Before I decided to write for the public's consumption, I took a short course on creative writing, read books written by other authors, and familiarized myself with different creative writing genres. However, although I was learning a lot about the technicalities of writing, there were realities of my culture, and particularities of the stories I wanted to tell, that were not considered in Western literature precepts. The best quote I have ever read is from Toni Morrison, "If there's a book you really want to read, but it hasn't been written yet, then you must write it." To me, it was as if one of my favorite writers, who was awarded the Nobel Prize for Literature in 1993, was permitting me to tell the stories of my people, the way they can be best narrated, even if it may mean breaking some rules.

If you would like to listen to gurus without necessarily allowing them to kill your creativity, this is what you should note:

- A guru is a source of knowledge and not of creativity. You are creative, and the guru is knowledgeable, and we do not necessarily find both in one basket.
- Fetch knowledge water from the guru, but do not ever let him/her spoil the soup you will make using his/her water. He/she may know nothing about spicing the soup.
- Consult a guru for insights, but not for approval! These are two different terms.
- It's important to be a guru in what you do, and that's why you should invest in acquiring knowledge and skills. You should also analyze your own experiences and make educated conclusions. Listening to the guru should be with the aim to learn, but not to seek for the guru's approval.

What gurus have in common is the fact that they became experts in their domains after a lot of persistence in whatever they did. They learned from their experiences, acquired and shared knowledge, and convinced the society that they mastered what they talked about. You shall only be able to win gurus to your side by learning to persist. I am not talking about being rigid; I am talking about being persistent. You should use the guru's knowledge to your advantage instead of letting the guru ruin your ability to get inspired, generate ideas, and use your intelligence and reasoning abilities to evaluate and visualize these ideas. How about other creativity killers? Let's look at the perfectionist.

The Perfectionist

Perfection is about the state of being too good so that nothing else could be better. It's different from excellence, which is the state of surpassing ordinary standards. Perfection is ideal and has never been achieved by any human being. Excellence is realistic and possible to achieve.

Creative people do not strive for perfection but excellence. When perfectionists judge our work, they look for flaws and faults and convince us that we cannot do it as long as it's not perfect. Unlike the guru who comes out knowledgeable, the perfectionist often does not comprehend how things are done. He/she looks for imperfections, without considering the production realities and challenges. A perfectionist strives for flawlessness and sets excessively high standards, often unrealistic. A perfectionist shall tell you that you can't sing if you don't do it better than Mozart or cannot be a painter if your paintings cannot compete with Da Vinci's. He/she does not acknowledge the difference between semi-finished products and finished products, or realize that the first lot may not be so good, but the second lot may be great. The perfectionist interprets mistakes as failure.

Because perfectionists never actually achieve perfection, they tend to doubt their ability to accomplish work beyond the ordinary, and keep on checking if any person around them can attain those high standards. When you have done some extraordinary work, perfectionists think you are unique, and to confirm their opinions of themselves, label you a genius, exceptional, or remarkably gifted. That conclusion gives them peace of mind that they did not achieve the high goals they set for themselves because they were not geniuses. Due to this kind of thinking, perfectionists shall criticize your work to remind you that what you're trying to do is only reserved for a few exceptionally gifted people. Perfectionists can kill creativity. They will attack it when it is still in the early stages of inspiration and idea generation.

The following is the best way to handle perfectionists to ensure they do not kill your creativity:

- First of all, never focus on getting their approval; they will always find a flaw in what you do;
- Whenever you receive criticism from a perfectionist, evaluate it objectively, but remember to focus on what you want to achieve and not the way he/she wants you to do things;
- Do not be defensive; you will push him/her to justify his/her position, and he/she might hurt and confuse you more. Stay cool and calm when responding to him/her. A nice "thank you" can do;
- Get positive feedback from other people; those who can recognize the efforts you have invest-

ed in what you have done, and realistically advise you on opportunities for improvement;
- Don't suffer from the noise of the perfectionists in the background. Decide when it's the right time to tell the perfectionist that you thank him/her for his/her feedback and that that should be all. You need no more input from him/her;
- Do not give up. Yes, he/she wants you to reach perfection in an unreal way. Remember, you are on the right track. You are moving from 'not so good' to 'good,' then to 'great,' to 'excellent' and, hopefully, to 'perfect.'

The Sponsor

The sponsor is one of the most dangerous creativity killers because he/she has the key to the gates you want to go through to achieve your success. A sponsor is a person you look up to for approval of your work, job offer, financial support, or that person who introduces you in whatever industry you want to enter.

For those that are formally employed by different organizations, sponsors are the decision-makers in the organization. For the movie scriptwriters and actors, sponsors may be the film producers and directors. For writers like me, sponsors may be publishers. We have sponsors everywhere. For university research associates, sponsors may be the professors who supervise their research work. For businesspeople, bankers may sometimes play the sponsor role.

Unlike gurus and perfectionists, sponsors can say, "You do it this way, or else, I will not allow you to do it." Sponsors may combine this role with being a guru, a perfectionist, or a lover, making them even more influential.

The gurus and perfectionists may criticize your creative ideas and try to convince you to give up. However, if you are not asking for their support, you may choose not to pay attention to them. On the other hand, sponsors shall demand that you consider their opinions; failure to do so may lead to their disapproval, hence withholding their support, which is essential for your creative endeavors.

The bad news is sponsors are investors, not necessarily of finances, but even their time, name, and support. Before sponsoring you, working with you, or associating their name with what you do, they always calculate what is in it for them, and if the risk is higher than the possible return, they disapprove of your work. As a creative person, you go through many trials and errors, and allow yourself to learn from your mistakes before you shall finally attain excellence. Unfortunately, the sponsor does not want to get involved at the stage of trials and errors. He/she wants to come in when he/she is sure his/her sponsorship won't be in vain.

Sponsors will never pursue you to discourage you from doing what you want. They shall silently observe how you invest time and effort in doing what you do, and it's when they will be proved you have what it takes to achieve the success that they shall decide to be part of it. The sponsor has only one objective: to share your success, but not the risks attached to your trials and errors. The good thing about sponsors is that even though it might take time to convince them, when they shall finally be convinced, they will open the gates of success for you as long as you shall allow them to enter them with you.

A lot of creative people ignore sponsors; you should not. You should manage them. Some clients can also play the role of sponsors. I remember when my brother Strong Karakire started to receive money for his art. He started from nothing. All he needed was a pencil and paper. Then he used to deliver his art to one big art shop in Kigali. They were not in frames, and he was paid very little money. The shop owner used to put them in lovely frames and sell them for a very high price. They were signed Strong Karakire, and everybody who visited that shop was amazed by the artist's talents. Today, that shop owner is one of the loyal clients of Strong Karakire. Do you know who sets the price now? Strong Karakire. He delivers finished products for a price he judges to be reasonable.

There is a crucial decision any writer has to make: how to publish his/her book. He/she has to choose between traditional publishing and self-publishing. Some authors decide to try traditional publishing and wait for the day a literary agent shall be interested in their work and convince a traditional publisher to take it. Some other authors choose self-publishing for its benefits, e.g., control over production, marketing, and sales. Most authors aspire to sign a deal with a traditional publisher one day but choose not to wait; instead, they start as self-published authors. Apparently, days are gone when the traditional publishers paid more attention to the literary content than the author's name. Days are gone when the author would be a person unknown to the general public till the day he/she would write a compelling story. Today, publishers are more concerned with how much they are likely to gain from the book deal than the quality of the written content. A celebrity or any other public figure, who already has followership of those who will love to read whatever he/she may write, is likely to sign a deal with a traditional publisher than an unsung author with a compelling and well-written story. If you're a writer, it would probably be best not to rely on literary agencies and renowned traditional publishers, and start as a self-publisher. When your books will be selling well, you shall not only sign deals with traditional publishers, you will have more bargaining power in negotiating how much they shall invest in the book deals.

The same applies to singers who do not wait to be picked by music record labels. They approach freelance audio and video producers to make their music before uploading it to available music streaming platforms online. As a creator, nothing or nobody should stop you from giving it a try. Don't worry; there will be a time, working with you shall be a privilege that many shall be looking forward to.

Even though you should not allow them to stop you, you need to learn how to work with sponsors?

- Win their hearts before winning their support. Sponsors do generally not support you because they want to help. They simply do that because of the gains they calculate from the deal. If you can, get them to move from their head to their heart. I do not mean you should maliciously manipulate them. I mean you should persuade them to embrace your vision and support you because they want to be part of it, and not because of the financial gain they may get from sponsoring you.
- Your aim should be to get them to fall in love with the cause you've devoted yourself to. If you fail to convince them with the 'what' and 'how', convince them with the 'why.'
- Treat them as partners and not sponsors. Listen to their pieces of advice; respect their opinions,

but continue to own the idea. Do not try to convince them that you are right. Instead, convince them that you are passionate about what you want to do.
- Be flexible. Give to receive. Sponsors shall come up with a list of changes you should make before they can be involved in what you do. If these are not so compromising, you can give it to them.
- Last and more importantly, whenever possible, think about ways to achieve your goals without any sponsor. You may start small, but assuredly. Sponsoring yourself shall not only save you time and resources; it will also allow you to keep the originality of your work.

In my home country, we have young unemployed people who complain about favoritism, capitalism, and everything else that makes it hard for them to make it in their lives. Some of them say that they completed their studies, have academic degrees, but have been waiting to get jobs for several years. When I ask them if they have never thought of starting a venture on their own, most of them tell me how hard it is to penetrate some markets and industries. It saddens me a lot to listen to stories of the young women subjected to sexual abuse and exploitation simply because they wanted to get an actress role in a movie or have a song produced by a record label. Some young men also have to pay bribes to get jobs or be allowed to penetrate some industries. My simple advice to them is that they should not surrender their key to success to anybody. They should learn to use capitalism to their advantage instead of being its victims. Below are examples of what they may do:

- Do not wait to write until you find a publisher; create a blog. Write an e-book that people can download from your blog and other sources. Do you have some money? Consider self-publishing.
- Do not wait to write a song and make a video until you have a music label. Write a song, record it, and upload it on the internet.
- Do not wait to do fashion designs until you buy a tailoring machine. Scissors, thread, and needles cost less.
- Do not wait to open up a shop in the city; you can sell online and deliver to your clients' houses.
- More importantly, start today and save for tomorrow.

It's good to have sponsors, but it's even better to start without them, so that those who will decide to be part of what you do, shall come because he/she has received your unique message, embraced your vision, and decided to be part of it. I encourage you to just start with what you can do and what you can afford. Let the sponsors discover you. Let them realize that working with you is as beneficial to them as it is to you. That's the only time you shall be able to sit at the table and bargain with the sponsors.

The Lover

This creativity killer is different from the others but

equally critical. The intentions of the lover are the best. A lover is a person dear to you. He/she might be your parent, sibling, spouse, boyfriend or girlfriend, or best friend. You trust this person and the last thing you want to do is doubt his/her judgment. You do not like the situation whereby, on the one hand, your heart tells you 'yes', and on the other, the person who usually is by your side says 'no.' You are afraid that if you do not listen to him/her, it may affect your relationship. It feels like you can never afford that.

However, there is some truth that you do not know, or you do not take into account. This person is only threatening to leave the relationship as his/her way of pushing you to reconsider your decision because he/she thinks you are going unsafe. Do you know why he/she thinks so? No. You don't. I also don't. All I know is that there could be different reasons. Maybe he/she is genuinely convinced that the risk involved in whatever you want to undertake is higher than the return. The second reason could be that he/she has lost hope and trust in the world and its people; he/she decided to survive on whatever the world offers him/her. He/she wants you to adopt that same pessimistic thinking. The third reason is that should you fly with your wings, he/she may lose control of you, which makes him/her uncomfortable. The fourth reason that is very common is that he/she has seen in you what he/she thinks is right and more acceptable, and believes what you want to do may make you a different person.

Creativity killers in this category of those I call 'lovers' have been the most challenging in my creative journey. These include my relatives, my best friends, and other people, who, I knew, appreciated me. Surprisingly, none of them has ever told me that what I do is wrong or useless. They all tell me that I am taking risks that I should not take. They are afraid that there could be people who do not want the stories I narrate to be told. Others think that visibility comes with challenges that I might not be prepared for. There are also those who tell me that even though what I do is commendable, I'm wasting my efforts and time because the world I want to change shall never change.

Normally it should not be a problem to listen to them, understand their concerns, and assure them that I will be okay. What becomes hard to comprehend is the fact that some of these people threaten to cut contact, put an end to our friendship, or, worse, abandon me. It hurts to be told by a relative that your relationship does no longer count because you chose to do things your way.

So many people find themselves in the same situation. These include those who are forced by their parents to pursue studies and specialize in the areas they are neither good at nor interested in. Some others are boyfriends, threatened to receive a "Dear John" because their girlfriends do not support what they want to venture into. Some spouses threaten to make the marriage a nightmare because they disapprove of the activities that their husbands or wives want to venture into. It's hard to deal with these creativity killers.

Most people give in because they want to save their friendship, relationship, or marriage. Family comes first, doesn't it? Some others choose not to listen. They pursue their creative endeavors despite the disapproval by their parents, siblings, relatives, friends, lovers, or spouses. The first years are usually a challenge. However, the friendship or the relationship that is meant to last does not usually break because you have chosen to be yourself.

Below are a few suggestions about handling these creativity killers:

- Win the heart before you win the argument: This may sound controversial because you know you have already won his/her heart. I am not referring to you winning his/her heart for you. I mean winning it for your interests.
- Do not only go to him/her to discuss decisions; start by just sharing interests. You should not pull him/her compellingly to what you like; be contagious in your sharing of interests and experiences.
- Speak his/her language: Is he/she usually logical. Speak logically and give him facts to sustain your position. Is he/she emotional? Speak emotionally, listen to his/her feelings, and assure him/her that all shall be well. You may confuse him/her by giving a lot of facts.
- Avoid discussing your relationship; focus on the matter: Never bring your relationship into the conversation. It should be kept intact. What you are talking about is your creative endeavors and the decisions you are making. It does not change the fact that you are still his/her child, sibling, spouse, or lover.
- Know when and how you agree to disagree: This may not come from him/her in most cases. You may be the one to say, "Honey, I love you, but once in our lives, I will disagree with you on this."
- Please keep in mind that your relatives and

friends are not necessarily your clients, fans, or followers. Do not sell to them. Let them discover what you do the same way everybody does. Don't be offended if they tell you they have never read your book, listened to your song, or don't like your paintings and whatever else you do.
- Remember, you do not owe them any explanation for things that do not concern them. For example, suppose I have written a story or a poem about my family. In that case, I might share it with my siblings before or after publication and respond to their questions for clarification. However, if it's a fiction story or a poem about my other conundrums, I may choose not to explain to them why I wrote what I wrote.

Self

In most cases, we are the ones that take a hummer and kill our creative potential. Our hummer is so severe because it has sharper teeth, which present themselves as our negative thoughts. In the first step of this quest to turn your creative potential into success, we discussed the situation that led to the conclusion that there is no reason to be creative. The following are some of the questions you asked yourself before you came to that conclusion:

- Where am I? How you view the world and its people, the opportunities given by this world, your appreciation of diversity, and the ability to live with it in harmony affect your thoughts and feelings about the world, influencing your decisions and actions.

- Is the world worth trusting? Your level of trust in people and their intentions affects your ability to interact with them, benefit from synergy with them, and leverage their ideas, talents, and moral support, to bridge to what you want to achieve.
- Am I allowed to be who I am? Your response to this question affects your ability to judge other people's opinions. It affects your ability to positively receive constructive feedback without being either defensive or submissive.
- To what extent am I allowed to make mistakes? Your response to this question affects your ability to dare, take risks, venture into different endeavors, and enjoy the experience. It also affects your ability to see mistakes as learning experiences and not a failure.

How do you handle this creativity killer 'self'? That's the purpose of this book, and the following are tips that you have already learned:

- Know yourself and never underestimate your abilities. You know what you can do and what challenges you.
- Formulate your life purpose and set your goals. This shall always motivate you to keep moving and never give up because you can see where you're heading and why.
- Yes, it's never going to be easy, and that's why you should devise your strategy. Instead of giving up, whenever you encounter difficulties, revisit your

strategy, and see where you should invest more time and effort.
- Think and act. Are you facing some challenges? Think about how to overcome them. Take action. Generate more creative ideas. Produce more. Re-package your products, and expand your distribution channels.
- Use your people networks to your advantage. Learn from both their words of encouragement and their criticisms. Learn from the gurus. Check the flaws the perfectionist is pointing fingers to and correct what you can. Find sponsors and convince them to be part of what you do. Ensure that even if you do not necessarily have the approval of your relatives and friends, you can always count on their love.
- Challenge yourself. Tell yourself you can. Reward yourself. Celebrate your success.

You have started producing creative products and put them out into the market. It has not been easy because you have and are still fighting with some creativity killers. There are voices in the background, including yours, that continue to tell you that you shall soon realize that you should not even have tried. However, you're also receiving some positive feedback. Some people are congratulating you. Others are buying your products. There are even those who have started to celebrate your success, even though you have a long way to go. In the next chapter, we shall discuss how to manage your success so that it won't be short-lived.

STEP 9

Celebrate Your Success

What is success?
Before we discuss success, let's look at its opposite, because our aim is actually to avoid it. I define failure as the state or condition of not meeting the intended or desirable objective. We, all of us, find ourselves in this state of failure at one point in time or another. I hear sentences such as; I have failed to catch my connecting train; I have failed to deliver on time; I have failed to make my soup the way I wanted. I have failed my school exam. I have failed the competition. The worst sentence I have ever heard, and any psychologist shall tell you that it's alarming, is: "My life is a failure."

Sometimes when we hear people saying that their life is a failure, we fail to understand them. How can they say their life is a failure when they are among the wealthiest people we know? How can they say their life is a failure when they have incredibly achieved academic success? How can they say their life is a failure when they are in good health? How can they say their life is a failure when they are alive? How dare they say their life is a failure? Do you know why? Because they never accomplished their life purpose and are seeing themselves leaving their world the same way they found it, or in some cases, worse than the way it was when they joined.

You have already defined your life purpose and have set goals to achieve in life. You shall not evaluate your success in terms of how many creative products you put out in the market. Your success is not determined by how many people know your name and how many followers you have on social media. You shall evaluate your success based on how far you have accomplished your life purpose and how you achieved your goals in all aspects of your life.

There are three elements that I call 3-S pillars of success, which we have briefly discussed in step 5: Self-realization, social connectedness, and social responsibility.

Self-realization

We all aspire to fulfill our potential, develop and apply our abilities to the maximum, be free from all sorts of boundaries, and be the best we can become. This affects how each of us thinks and feels about him/herself. It's about the social status each of us wants to achieve in society. Some people want to be in the circles of the most educated and intellectual. Others want to be famous and in the gatherings of celebrities. Others want to be politically influential. Others want to be rich and wealthy. We invest our time and effort in making sure we reach the heights of our success. We think we shall be happier and healthier when we shall have gained the social status we aspire for.

However, when some people become wealthier, famous, and more influential, they realize it does not always guarantee wellbeing and happiness. Do you know why? Because when formulating their life purpose and setting their goals, they did not take into consideration all aspects of their life: Physical, emotional, intellectual, spiritual, and financial.

Many creative people, such as writers, musicians, artists, and others, invest a lot in turning their creative potential into success. However, when their definition of success is limited to becoming rich and famous, they often live miserable lives. Having a lot of money is indeed an indicator of financial success. However, though very important, money does not buy everything, as some people like to say. My advice to all creative people is to evaluate their success in all aspects of their life. Does it make you a happier person? (Emotional) Are you becoming more enlightened? (Intellectual) Are you more connected to existence and immortality? (Spiritual) Are you healthier and safer? (Physical) Do you invest your earnings in projects that lead to more sustainable economic abundance? (Economic). Other people may evaluate your success based on what they see. They will even compare you with others, and you might feel discouraged when your name is not on the list of the wealthiest, most famous, or most influential. Please bear in mind that what you aim for is not a success in one aspect of your life, but balanced success in all aspects.

Social connectedness

You may be successful in what you do as an individual.

However, you should remember that you are a social being. Your success shall not be complete if your relationships and connections with other people in your family, community, and society are not in good shape. You should learn to balance your goals for self-realization with those of social connectedness. The time or other resources you spend interacting with other people, helping others, and sharing their joy and pain is not wasted. As a human, you will never be as happy and safe as you should be if you do not have quality relationships with other people.

However, even though other people are excellent sources of encouragement, they are also sources of discouragement. We go to other people to seek comfort and advice, but sometimes we find ourselves somehow in loathsome situations with people. People are consumers and supporters of our creative products. But, on the other hand, people seem not to understand us. They discourage us when we want to fly our wings. Yes, they give us, but they also take from us. Nevertheless, it does not matter whether people are friendly to you or not. Whether you like it or not, you are connected to other people and should take care of that social connectedness. Any attempt to disconnect from other people can only harm and hurt you.

As we discuss social connectedness, I would like to introduce two other concepts: Social Capital and Social Trust. There are many definitions of social capital. I want to define it as "the advantage of being part of the social networks of people who are ready and willing to do things for each other." On the other hand, social trust is a belief in the honesty, integrity, and reliability of others. To be successful, we need both social capital and social trust. Most successful people might be surrounded by crowds and be known by many people, but without having built a reliable social network of people who are willing to be there for them, irrespective of the happenings in their lives. Many experts shall tell you what you should do to build useful social capital for your success. All I will say to you is that you should instead identify your natural social networks and make sure you do not destroy the social capital you already have.

What do I mean? In pursuit of success, we meet people who seem to be more excited about what we do than our relatives, longtime friends, and members of the communities, of which we are natural members. However, we should keep in mind that our relationships with these people may not have yet reached the social trust that is the cornerstone of any social capital. If you are a musician, you shall realize it the day you shall stop singing or when your music shall no longer be among the top. When you shall no longer be invited to walk on the red carpet or take the flow to speak in conferences, you shall realize that social capital does not mean being surrounded by many people who excitedly shout out your name.

I advise you to stay connected to your family members, even those who disapprove of your creative endeavors. I encourage you to be part of the community activities in your neighborhood. As you expand your business networks, do never forget your friends, especially your longtime friends. Be intentional in keeping quality relationships with those people who believe in your integrity and honesty. I mean those who may not necessarily see you as a hero, but have faith in you.

Since the publication of my debut novel and my poetry, I have gained new friendships and subscribed to networks of people that I could probably not have met if I had not voiced my opinions on some topics. However, what I have so far realized is that these people do not know me well, irrespective of how much I share with them. They only judge what I say or do, without having the full picture of who I am. They have not yet reached the level of trusting my honesty and integrity. Anything I say or do may make them feel more connected with me or disconnect with me. I'm getting used to that. I no longer feel rejected when a supporter decides to cut contact with me, or when I regretfully take the decision to cut contact with a person or withdraw from a group. What matters most is how I maintain the trust of those who are naturally part of my social capital, as I connect with other people who trust my honesty and integrity. Your relationship with people who matter more in your life is key. Please, do not trade it for anything else.

Social responsibility

If you never want to be asking yourself the question of "so what" when you will be approaching the end of your journey on this earth, think about what you should do that the whole world can benefit from. Through these deeds, you will live millions of years after we cease shaking hands with you. That's how you will achieve the success that is not short-lived; success that continues to prosper even after your death.

After making millions of dollars in their life, many people feel like, "What was I running after? What purpose was I serving?" Some of them shall start engaging in philanthropy. Others shall write memoirs and autobiographies. Some other people amend their will and give a big part of their assets to the poor. All these are great decisions, but it's not what I'm talking about here. I want to remind you of your life purpose, the bigger cause you chose to serve, and the contributions you aimed to make to our world's betterment.

Unlike social connectedness, social responsibility goes beyond what you do for your family, neighborhood, or community. It is about what you do for society at large. It's about how everything you say or do contributes to solving the most critical problems, not only of your city or country but the world's societies at large. For example, if you decide to do something to address climate change, you will be contributing to something beneficial to all living beings. The same applies to a decision to address the world's issues such as racism, tribalism, ethnicism, violence, etc. You might choose to contribute to poverty reduction or eradication by either helping the poor or supporting economic development efforts. There is a lot you might decide as a socially responsible person.

However, you should note that social responsibility is more about the science of being than the art of giving. It's about your ethics, as a citizen of the world. As a socially responsible person, you have obligations to fulfill. You pay your taxes. You abide by both national and universal laws. You exercise your rights and respect the rights of others. You live in harmony with the diversity that surrounds you. Some people pursue success in their lives, but forget that if this world we all call our home is not taken care of, we shall all perish. Social responsibility is about living responsibly.

What is success, and how is it achieved?

- You shall achieve success by fulfilling your potential to be the best you can be in your life; physical, emotional, intellectual, spiritual, and financial. (Self-realization)
- You shall achieve success through creating and maintaining quality relationships with your family, friends, neighbors, colleagues, community members, compatriots, and other world citizens. The more social capital and social trust you enjoy, the more successful you are. (Social-connectedness)
- You shall achieve success through the ethical fulfillment of your obligations as a socially responsible world citizen, by solving society's problems as large. (Social responsibility)

Why and how to celebrate success

Celebrating your success is recognizing that you have achieved one short-term goal, then another one, and another one, and so on. It's about applauding the steps you make towards accomplishing your life purpose. Why should you do that? I will probably ask you why people celebrate calendar events such as New Years', birthdays, wedding anniversaries, and other sorts of things. My understanding is that when we celebrate milestones, we give ourselves the opportunity to review what we have so far accomplished, and vow to do more or better than we did the day, week, month, or the year before. Celebrating your success is communicating that you have not only made some steps, but are still committed to making even more steps towards achieving your goals.

Below are the few reasons why you should celebrate success:

- Celebrating success gives you an opportunity to signal the goals you have so far achieved;
- It gives you confidence that things are not as challenging as they seem;
- It makes the experience to work toward accomplishing your life purpose more exciting and enjoyable;
- It gives you the opportunity to express gratitude to those who supported you along the way;
- It motivates you to stay on the journey towards fulfilling your life purpose.

When you celebrate your success, you should always evaluate the following:

- Merit: Do your achievements deserve to be celebrated? Did you achieve your short-term goals? Did you achieve your long-term goals? Were you committed to work hard? Did you give all you had to make sure you succeed in your creative endeavors?
- Worth: What was the quality of your work? How well did you achieve your goals? How useful are your creative products? If you were to celebrate it the same way soccer teams do, would you celebrate it the same way they do after scoring a goal by just jumping, kissing, and then go on with work? Or you would celebrate it the same way

they do when they win a national championship or a world cup?
- Significance: Are you celebrating the achievement of goals that lead to the accomplishment of your life purpose? What impact have you made in yourself, your family, your community, and society? What's the opportunity cost you paid, and how do you compare that cost to the return?

I am a fun-loving person who encourages people always to celebrate the gift of life and this should be for every hour and every minute. However, there is a misconception about celebrating success.

Two months into our marriage, my husband and I decided to sit down and set goals about what we needed to achieve as a couple and family. We came up with three goals we vowed to achieve in three years. We drew a budget and started saving money towards the achievement of our goals. During the three years, we were able to attain two of the goals that we had set. It was not easy. We had had to forgo some leisure that we believed we were entitled to as young as we were. I remember one Friday when I closed my office, trying to rush home. My work colleagues were standing outside, waiting to go out to spend money and have fun. Then when I passed by them and said, "Goodbye friends," one of them, a tall, handsome guy, said, "Where are you going? Why do you live that boring life? Can't you join us and have fun?" I looked at him, smiled at him, and said, "Have a nice weekend." What he had said was not entirely true because my husband and I did not at all have boring lives. However, we aimed high enough not to waste our money on drinks and brochettes in Kigali bars.

Today, going out to a bar or restaurant does not longer seem expensive compared to the level of our earnings. However, I still receive questions similar to what my former colleague asked me. Some people ask me why I drive a particular car model and not the other. Others ask why I live in a particular neighborhood and not the other. Whenever I say that I cannot afford some car models, smart telephones, or the houses they think I should own, they tell me that the problem is that I am probably frugal. I don't think I am too thrifty. I simply recognize the fact that I have not yet realized many of my long-term goals. Yes, I have won some games and achieved some goals. I have celebrated that level of success the way it should be celebrated because I have not yet won the championship. Sometimes I achieve some long-term goals, but there is still a long way to go before accomplishing my life purpose.

We have understood the importance of celebrating success, but the question is about how we celebrate it.

Below are a few tips on how you may celebrate your achievements, without spending a fortune:

- Make a list of all your achievements based on the indicators you defined when you set your goals. This shall give you a perfect sense of how you are moving towards accomplishing your purpose. Whenever you look at this list, clap for your success.
- Write a success story about yourself, your experiences, your successes, and the lessons learned on the way. I do this, and I can tell you that after writing it, you feel like reading it more times, and

then you feel more committed to seeing your story evolving to something bigger.
- Share the news with your partners, friends, and family. This is the best way to reward those who support your work and encourage more people to be part of what you do. Let them be part of your success.
- Write a gratitude letter to everyone who supported you. When you do this, it communicates that you recognize that other people encouraged you and that you are grateful. It also gives you the opportunity to celebrate your social capital.
- Keep a success journal. It helps you keep track of the steps you are making and the milestones you are going through.
- Reward yourself with something you like. It does not have to be expensive but memorable. Something that shall remind you that you earned it. I sometimes buy a bottle of champagne and celebrate with my family whenever my work is published or gets positive feedback.

I congratulate you on having made significant steps towards turning your creative potential into success. After discovering your potential, you entered the workshop to generate creative ideas and products. When you put them out to the market, you received both positive and negative feedback, including discouragements that we have defined as creativity killers. You have fought the battle with creativity killers and have won. Now you are recording and celebrating success in all the pillars of your life; self-realization, social connectedness, and social responsibility. Maybe you are at a stage where you're already thinking about the legacy you would leave behind when you shall eventually close eyes forever now. That takes you to step 10, which is about putting your signature on the future.

STEP 10

Put Your Signature on the Future

Two things motivated me to write about this. The first one is the fact that I am a daughter to my parents, a granddaughter to my grandparents, a great-granddaughter to my great-grandparents. The second is that I am a mother who is alive today, but who may not be alive tomorrow. As a daughter, I keep so many good memories of my parents and a few memories of my grandparents. I have no memories of my great grandparents and those before them. When I look at my children, I see another generation and many more future generations of those who will want to know about and learn from us who are living today. These are generations that shall either be inspired by what we are doing today or disappointed by how we shall probably have destroyed the world. I would love my name to be mentioned by future generations for what I shall have done and achieved when I was alive, and be inspired by my contributions. That's why in everything I do, I want to think about my legacy.

I have been fortunate to be part of the generation that has access to free information. All you do is write some keywords in any of the internet search engines and find information about some alive or dead people who left a mark on the world. Interestingly, we also get information about some of the people who left this world long before the internet invention. They never used social media to publicize themselves. They had neither websites nor blogs to promote themselves. What made their names famous is what they did and how it affected other people in their surroundings. Yes, there were other communication channels, especially the mouth-to-ear, but information sharing was not as fast as today. These people are referred to even by current generations because what they did in the past is relevant even in the present, and shall probably continue to be relevant even in the future.

The people that I am talking about include inventors like Sir Isaac Newton (1642–1726), Albert Einstein (1879–1955), and William George Armstrong (1810–1900). The list includes artists like Leonardo da Vinci (1452–1519). It includes those who did incredible humanitarian acts like Mother Teresa (1910–1997). It includes revolutionists, politicians, and civil activists like Mahatma Gandhi (1869–1948), Nelson Mandela (1918-2013), and Martin Luther King Jr. (1929–1968). The list can go on.

I recognize that there are similar names of those who left their signature on the future in different cultures and parts of the world. We read about some of them on the internet. Some other names are not found on the internet, but their stories are still told today in their communities.

What did these people do that made their names stay engraved not only on their tombstones but also in the world's memory? Some of them did something that proved expertly using intelligence and changed the way we do things today. Some others contributed by helping the underprivileged, and they did it with love and devotion in a way that inspires many. Others risked their lives because of their courage to be a voice of the voiceless and a fighter for rights of the less powerful.

Even today, some people are putting their signature on the future. Although I will probably not witness when future generations shall be referring to their experiences as life lessons, I commend them for the legacies they want to leave behind, from which our descendants shall learn a lot.

Are you one of those who are putting a signature on the future? What does your signature look like? Let's look at three types of signatures.

Signature of excellence

This is about what you did. It's the 'What' you did in your life that was judged excellent by others. The truth is that today it's even harder to earn recognition for excellence. You may be able to have your names searchable on the internet, but that won't mean that you will have done something great and excellent. Today, instead of focusing on producing creatively excellent work, it seems that many people choose to recycle what the world is already familiar with and promote their ability to do things like anybody else. Nowadays, some people express more the desire for fame than the desire to leave an impactful legacy. All they do is publicizing their name and making sure it is mentioned as many times as possible in different online and offline platforms. That's not what I am encouraging you to do. I am talking about the value you add to whatever you do, so it's distinguishable from what's done by other ordinary people. For example, if you are an architect, is your quest to design houses and buildings that shall help us overcome the climate change challenge? If you are a computer scientist, do you aim at developing hardware or software that shall make our daily businesses easier? If you are an artist, do you use your art to tell meaningful stories and encourage this world's citizens to appreciate the beauty and the diversity that surround us?

Today there are so many products out there, and some people think there is nothing more to add to what is already available. Their contribution is limited to mastering what is already in place and use it the way it was meant to be used. In schools, we are taught more about what is already known, and little effort is spent on encouraging us to explore the unknown and create something new out of it. Creative people use their ability to generate novel ideas that can lead to both inventions and innovations. Inventors find something existent and identify how it can be used for different purposes. On the other hand, innovators build from what is already there and add a feature that changes it and makes it even more useful.

Putting a signature of excellence on the future is done by those who understand that the fact that something is good does not necessarily mean it's excellent. They continuously question how things are done and search for opportunities for improvement. They believe that those who lived before us came up with innovations and inventions that changed the world to what we enjoy today and that we should add our value and make the world better than how we found it.

Do you want your name to be remembered for what you excellently did? Be creative, professional, and excellent in whatever you do. What matters is not only why you do what you do, but also how you do what you do. Are you a creative writer, do it exceptionally well so that it is comparable to the works of the laureates of the Nobel Prize for literature. Are you a singer? Don't only rely on having a beautiful voice; learn all the techniques for singing, and make sure you sing professionally well. In everything you do, make sure you do it better than how it has been done before by either yourself or others. Always find opportunities for improvement, and make sure what you do is not only acceptable but excellent.

Signature of inspiration

Unlike the signature of excellence, which is about 'what' you did well, this signature of inspiration is about how you lived in whatever you engaged in. When I grow older, I will love to hear my daughters responding to one of the most common questions: "Who inspired you?" and then they shall say, "Our mother was a great source of inspiration for us." That's when I shall be looking forward to kissing goodbye to this world and going for a peaceful eternal rest. Although it's possible, I do not think my children will be talking about the fact that I'm an excellent writer. I don't think they will be talking about the jobs I held and what a great performer I was. They will be talking about how my values, behaviors, and deeds influenced how they think, feel, and act in their own lives. They will be saying that they do what they do because of what I did, how I did it, and why I did it.

Some people are recognized for excellence in what they did. However, this does not always mean that other people are willing to follow their steps. To inspire another person, he/she should see you as a role model, and a lot of parameters come into play. People shall not only be inspired by your ability to create new things excellently, but also how whatever you do, even in other areas of your life, makes them want to be like you.

You have heard different people questioning why the media and the public are interested in both the professional and personal lives of public figures, such as politicians, artists, and successful businesspeople. The media or some members of the public would often respond, "As a public figure who serves the world, your personal life becomes a business of all of us who are affected in one way or the other by what you do."

A person, who inspires others, seeks excellence in all aspects of his/her life, ensures good relationships with others, and acts as a responsible world citizen.

Do you want to put a signature of inspiration on the future? Below are ideas of what you shall have done to inspire others:

- You have used your creativity not only to come up with novel ideas and products but those that shall change the lives of many people;
- Your story, your words and deeds, changed the lives of those who lived during your time, and those of the future generations;
- You have lifted other people to where you are,

and inspired them to be better than you, and reach even higher heights.
- You inspired others, not only because you were the most genius and influential person in the world, but because you endeavored to do better every day, despite the challenges you faced.
- You did not only probably achieve wonders, but aimed at achieving something more impactful and useful to all the world's citizens.

Some people might be great singers, artists, humanitarians, politicians, businesspeople, etc. However, that does not guarantee anybody will want to be like them, especially if what they did was detrimental to their well-being in other aspects of life, social usefulness, or responsibility. As Maya Angelou rightly said, "People will forget what you said, people will forget what you did, but people will never forget how you made them feel." As I encourage you to excel in whatever you do, and sign excellence on the future, I also urge you to think about what other people should learn from your story, especially why and how you say and do whatever you say or do.

Signature of purpose

We have heard of the stories of the people who pursued a greater purpose than what the world could immediately comprehend. Most of these were jailed or killed before they could even accomplish their purpose. Others are still alive, but they had to wait to see their actions credited to be extraordinary, years after they decided to defend a cause and accomplish a purpose that was bigger than them. During those times, everyone could wonder why they were investing efforts and energy in risking their lives. However, today whenever their names are mentioned, they are no longer labeled as rebels or prisoners but heroes. Do you know why they were labeled as rebels? It's not because they took guns and kill innocents. Those are not the ones I am talking about. Most of these people asked themselves the "why" question. They questioned why things were going the way they were. Why were African Americans marginalized? Why was colonization accepted as normal? Why did black South Africans not have the same rights as their fellow white South Africans? Why did some Rwandans not have the right to live in their own country?

The people I'm talking about do not need to be only political revolutionists or human rights activists. We know those known as significant people because they believed in the truth that can save the world and pursued that truth. These include any person who has decided to change the world dynamics because he/she believed we all need to make the world better for all of us and future generations. Those who spoke about peace when everybody else was singing war songs. Those who spoke about love standing at the crossroads of communities antagonized by hatred. Those who did not curse prisoners, poor people, or any other groups of people our world chooses to condemn and blame. Most of these people did not have any other objective apart from doing the right thing even when everybody else has chosen to do the opposite.

Maybe you don't see a clear link between what they did and creativity. You may be a writer like me, a singer, a poet, a visual artist, a mathematician, a politician, a humanitarian, or engaged in any other profession; you should always define your 'why.' That's what we have discussed in step 5 on formulating your life purpose and setting your goals. Your 'why' shall push you to think on more creative ways to make an impact. Many people are writers, but with different purposes. What makes Nadine Gordimer, the South African writer, Toni Morrison, the American writer, and Chinua Achebe, the Nigerian writer, distinguishable from other writers, is not only their literary excellence, but the purpose of their writing. Bob Marley was a great singer, no doubt about that. However, he is not only praised for his beautiful voice and the internationalization of the reggae music, but more importantly the revolutionary impact of his music.

These people started with the belief that the world could be better than it was, and today we call them our heroes because we have indeed seen what they were talking about. These people could see the end in their minds, and that pushed them to persist. Some of them strategized and generated ideas on how to go about accomplishing their purpose. Some of these people were creative thinkers and applied some novel and useful ideas to put their dreams into reality. My aim is neither to assess their creativity nor to encourage you to be like them. My objective is to let you understand that you should remember to stamp your signature on the future in whatever you do. One of the ways you may do it is with a signature of purpose.

To conclude, in this book, we have discussed how you should turn your creative potential into success. However, you should always bear in mind that life is short, and the only way you can eternalize it is by leaving a memorable mark on this world. It might be how excellent you did whatever you did, how you exemplarily lived your life in a way that is neither detrimental to your life nor the lives of others, or the fact that you aimed at making this world a better place of all the world's citizens. What shall you be remembered for?

Conclusion

This book's purpose was to take you through the process of turning your creative potential into success. Below are the steps you may have taken. If not, I will advise you to.

- Step #1: Assess your situation: What makes you view the world the way you do? When, how, and why did you lose trust in the world and its people? How did you develop the idea that you are not allowed to be yourself? How and when did you develop the idea that you are not allowed to make mistakes? Go back to the past and mentally undo the negative marks you have drawn on your brain as a result of some of your unpleasant experiences. Start fresh and be ready to rediscover yourself.
- Step #2: Discover your mental abilities: In the quest to rediscovering yourself, you will understand that you have more capabilities than you put at work. You will learn that you do not need to fit in people's definitions of intelligence that are usually not very right. You will understand

your level of intelligence and how it is translated into different mental abilities.
- Step #3: Understand your personality: It's all about how you think, feel, and act. Your personality traits are partly genetic and partly environmentally affected. By understanding your personality traits, you shall be able to emphasize those that push you towards creativity and control the behaviors that may result from the personality traits you want to keep tolerable.
- Step #4: Define your motivation factors: Your interests and the beauty of doing what you are interested in. Your strong desire to do what you do or want to do. The needs you try to satisfy when you do what you do. This understanding shall lead you to make decisions to change your situation, put your abilities at work, and adopt behaviors that shall lead you to success.
- Step #5: Define your life purpose and set your goals. After understanding yourself and making sure that you will change your situation, it's time for you to decide what you want to accomplish in life and set your ultimate, long-term, and short-term goals.
- Step #6: Draw your strategies: Now that you understand what you want to achieve, it's time to put in place the stones you will step on in order to achieve your goals and accomplish your life purpose.
- Step #7: Embark on creative production: It will all be real and actual when you will start to tap into your creative potential to generate ideas,

engage in a creative process to produce creative products, and finally supply the world with products of your creativity.
- Step #8: Fight with creativity killers: When you start getting out of the box, there are so many people who shall pull you back in. You should know how to handle these people in such a way that you benefit from the relationships you have with them without jeopardizing your decision and ability to get out of the box and turn your creative potential into success.
- Step #9: Congratulations! You are on the journey! Keep moving! Learn to celebrate your successes. Celebrate the achievement of goals related to your self-realization, social connectedness, and social responsibility. Celebrate your progress!
- Step #10: Put your signature on the future: It may be the signature of excellence, the signature of inspiration, or signature of purpose.

Supplemental Readings

Books

Amabile, T. (1983). *The Social Psychology of Creativity*. New York, NY: Springer-Verlag.

Csikszentmihalyi, M. (1996). *Creativity: Flow and the Psychology of Discovery and Invention*. New York, NY: HarperCollins Publishers.

Fishkin, A. et al. (Eds), *Investigating Creativity in Youth*. NJ: Hampton Press.

Gardner, H. (1993). *Frames of Mind: The Theory of Multiple Intelligences*. New York, NY: Basic Books.

Simonton, D.K. (1999). *Origins of Genius: Darwinian Perspectives on Creativity*. New York, NY: Oxford University Press.

Sternberg, R.J. (Ed.), *The Nature of Creativity*. New York, NY: Cambridge University Press.

Sternberg, R.J. (Ed.), *Handbook of Creativity*. Cambridge, England: Cambridge University Press.

Articles

Barron, F., & Harrington, D.M. (1981). Creativity, intelligence, and personality. Annual Review of Psychology, 32, 439-476.

Batey, M. & Furnham, A. (2006). Creativity, intelligence, and personality: A critical review of the scattered literature. Genetic, Social and General Psychology Monographs, 132, 355-429.

Chavez-Eakle, R.A. (2004). On the neurobiology of the creative process, Bulletin of Psychology and the Arts, 5, 29-35.

MacKinnon, D.W. (1962). The nature and nurture of creative talent, America Psychologist, 17, 484-95.

Richards, R., et al (1988). Assessing everyday creativity. Journal of Personality and Social Psychology, 54, 476-485.

Baum, J.R., & Locke, E.A. (2004). The relationship of entrepreneurial traits, skill, and motivation to subsequent venture growth. Journal of Applied Psychology, 89, 587-598.

www.ingramcontent.com/pod-product-compliance
Lightning Source LLC
Chambersburg PA
CBHW021146080526
44588CB00008B/231